The Momentum Journey

Break down at Exit 63

A BOOK ABOUT PERSISTENCE, PASSION, AND PERSEVERANCE DESIGNED TO INSPIRE THOSE IN NEED OF INSPIRATION.

Rob Lohman

MOJO Publishing, A Division of The Momentum Journey

The Momentum Journey :
Breakdown at Exit 63
By Rob Lohman

Published by:
MOJO Publishing, A Division of The Momentum Journey
P.O. Box 4238
Edwards, CO 81632 U.S.A.
(970) 331-4469
books@themomentumjourney.org
http://www.themomentumjourney.org/

Library of Congress Control Number: 2005930360

ISBN 0-9771337-0-2

Printed in the United States of America by United Graphics in Mattoon, IL

"Today, well lived, makes every yesterday a dream of happiness and every tomorrow a vision of hope."

- Sanskrit Proverb

Table of Contents

Acknowledgements

Mom and Dad

Your unconditional love for me is a story to be told in itself.   You provided me with an incredible college education, although I chose to receive a societal education. You loved me when I felt unlovable. You supported me when I took advantage of your kindness. Through no fault of your own, I fell into a world of confusion and lost identity.   I let the pressures of today's society lead me down the path most taken.

You introduced me to a loving God as a child which I chose to call upon only in desperate times later in life. That Godly seed you planted in my early years has grown into the most incredible guiding force in my life today. I had to go through every storm in my life to see the beauty on the other side. And I will say that this life is beyond beauty, beyond description, and beyond comprehension.

Thank you for letting me go when I was near my bottom in life because that truly saved my life. Thank you for your love. Thank you for my brother Eric and my dog Jake. Thank you. Thank you. Thank you.

xoxoxoxoxoxoxoxo   Love, Your Son Robbie

Barbara Hill

Words cannot express my gratitude for how you changed my life. Your caring soul and love for helping people discover their true calling in life must have been divinely inspired. You pulled me out of career disaster and revealed to me a life beyond imagination. You were the catalyst in the discovery of my newfound passion. Everyone needs someone like you as an influence in their lives. Thanks Barbara.

Bill Finley

Thank you for your guidance into the spiritual realm of life. You showed me the importance of looking at my entire life under a microscope. You taught me about my defects of character that shut me off from the sunlight of the Spirit for so long. You showed me who I really am. For that I am grateful. For that I can never repay you except to share with others what you so freely shared with me. Thanks Bill.

Melanie Gideon and Aric Geesaman

Both of you took a chance to help me fulfill my dreams while helping yourself during your own self-discovery journey. Your humor, positive outlook, willingness to live life, and uplifting spirit will always live on with me. We endured tough times together but learned valuable lessons along the way. I have faith that both of you will find your true calling in life if you continue to explore your options. Again, thank you.

Amy Brugh

God placed you in my life for inspiration. Your enthusiasm to enjoy each day is contagious. Your optimistic outlook makes it impossible to look at a glass as partially empty. Thank you for propelling The Momentum Journey to the next level. Thanks Amy for being (as you say) "my number one fan".

God

Thank you for sending your only Son to die for my sins. You allowed me to exhaust my own free will to discover a life beyond deserving. You had my life planned before I arrived on Earth. Most of the time I do not like your plan for me, but I accept it with grace and humility. I walk with you every moment of every day. I wake with you to these prayers upon my knees followed by moments of meditation:

> "God, grant me the serenity to accept the things I cannot change, the courage to change the things I can, and the wisdom to know the difference."

> "God, I offer myself to Thee— to build with me and to do with me as Thou wilt. Relieve me of the bondage of self, that I may better do Thy will. Take away my difficulties, that victory over them may bear witness to those I would help of Thy Power, Thy Love, and Thy Way of life. May I do Thy will always!"

Thanks God.

Friends and other believers

You keep the momentum moving forward. Thank you for your support.   Without you, The Momentum Journey would not exist.

I would like to especially thank the following 2004 Level D sponsors:

The Mike Colby Family, Aric Geesaman, Melanie Gideon, Bill Hackett, Dave & Andrea Lohman, Jim & Sally Lohman, Pete Lohman, Pat & Jen Thompson

AND

Level E sponsors:

David Banks, Greg Brubaker, Scott Ensley, Kevin & Deb Eskew, The Gibson Family, David Greigo, Tina Griffith, Gretchen Hernley, Adam Kerr, Klaiber's Sewing Center, Lowe's-Bloomington, IN, Amy Lukowski, Rebecca Martinez, Dave Naftzger, Jeremy Podany, Roy and Melissa Ritter, Katie Schlichter, Scott Shimster, and Mary Umstead.

Introduction

The Momentum Journey : Breakdown at Exit 63 is a true story of persistence, perseverance, and passion. It is about peaks and valleys. It is about expectations and disappointments. It is about hope and humility. It is about having a dream, a purpose, and a drive to succeed no matter what the obstacles may be. It is a story guided by the principles of faith. It is about a journey…The Momentum Journey.

~~~~~~

I wrote this book to help inspire people who feel trapped and are struggling to find their purpose in life. This book is like a set of tools for life that can be used and reused, actually sharpening with each use. I want people to look beyond what they know to learn what they do not know. After all, the day we stop learning is the day we stop living.

Fear is an emotion that does not discriminate.

It is up to each individual to find their spark and their passion, to leave their comfort zones and grow from their fears, and to go out to do great things. It is up to each individual to discover the hope that lies deep inside their soul and to live out their own dreams.
So why is that so many people in the world struggle to find their purpose in life? Who is the deciding factor in defining your purpose? Is it you? Your parents? Society? God's will? Your circle of influence? The wealthy neighbor? The poor neighbor? Who then?

Why is it that the average worker changes careers six times? Not jobs, but careers! Factor in a few jobs within each career and you are looking at an individual who is searching for their purpose. Have the days of long-term employment come and gone? Is your job security threatened? Are you fulfilled at work?

What is IT that makes people happy, joyous, and free? Is it a big house? A shiny car? A beautiful spouse? Successful children? A huge 401K? A quality relationship with your family? A balanced life? A relationship with a Higher Power of your understanding? A life with meaning and purpose?

Take a moment to reflect on some of the questions above and assess where you are today. I have found this tool extremely helpful in my career journey and I am sure you will too. How do you know where you are going if you don't know how you got where you are?

The stories you are about to read are real. They are about individuals who made life-changing sacrifices to pursue their passions in life. They are about the inspirations in your local communities. They are about finding a purpose in life.

Enjoy the book!

Gratefully,

Rob "The MOJO Man" Lohman

Warning: This book has not been professionally edited. All editing was conducted by yours truly. Read at your own risk! Proceed with caution.

Section 1 ..... My Story

I believe it is important to understand the stepping-stones which lead me to write this book and perhaps lead you to read this book. I can guarantee you one thing...this book will make you think about why you are where you are today. Ralph Waldo Emerson said "Make the most of yourself, for that is all there is of you." Is this true in your life?

Section 2 ..... What it was like

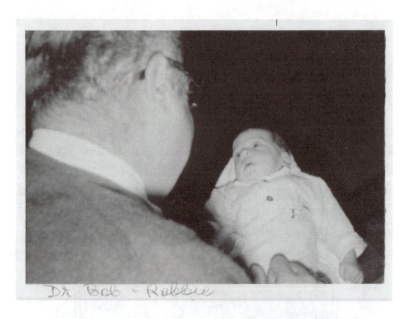

Dr. Bob - Robbie

Ever since my grandfather, Dr. Robert H. Lohman (a.k.a. Dr. Bob), delivered me into this world in 1971, I dreamed of helping people and of becoming a family doctor, just like him. I would spend hours hanging around Dr. Bob's office flirting with his nurses, spinning on his silver-legged, black cushioned "doctor's" chair, playing with the cold stethoscopes, and observing my grandfather enhance people's lives. Some days I imagined his patients acted sick so they could spend time with their favorite family doctor.

Whenever I visit Fort Wayne, IN as an adult, I always run into someone that says Dr. Bob delivered them or their kids or their kids' kids. My childhood dream was to be just like my grandfather.

Unfortunately that childhood dream slowly faded away when I attended college. I became less focused on academia and more focused on the social freedoms that college offered. My desire to be accepted by all stemmed from my insecurities as a child and the desire to feel "apart of" instead of "apart from". I was your best friend, but a stranger to myself. This enabled me to become a chameleon in any social circle, therefore I never really developed my own identity. To live a life based on other peoples' opinions is an empty life. Believe me, I know. Can you relate?

Friends of mine would always say to me "Lohman, I could drop you into a room full of strangers and you would come out with a handful of friends. What a gift!" Was it? I became who I needed to become so you would invite me into your circle.

Alcohol* created an outlet for me to forget my true identity. What an awesome freedom. Right? Wrong. The crazy thing is that alcohol created a temporary relief from my current problems and insecurities, but when I woke up in the morning those problems and insecurities were still present and sometimes worsened. I am grateful that this is not the case today as you are reading this book.

*refer to Appendix AA

After four years I somehow graduated from DePauw University in 1994 with a Bachelor of Arts in Biology. Having no idea what I wanted to do with my life I did what any other sensible lost student would do......headed to Vail, Colorado to "find myself".

I can say that this decision did not please many people, but it was something I had to do for me. While in Vail, I found myself alright. I found myself more confused than ever and even more directionless on how to determine a future career. After eighteen months in the "false reality" world of the Vail Valley I decided to move back to Texas to utilize the network of my family to find a job. Not a career, but something to help pay the bills.

The next five years were quite interesting: eighteen months as a personal banker ($19K), then two months as a property manager ($28K), then jointly started an MBA program at the University of Texas at Dallas and a career in commercial real estate for twenty-six months ($45K), then moved to Fort Wayne, Indiana for a new career in commercial real estate for twenty-one months ($65K)...... and then I said WHOA! I realized that I had been in commercial real estate for over four years, but commercial real estate was not in me. Something had to change. AND IT DID!

Section 3 ..... What happened

During a fishing trip in Indiana with some college buddies a seed was planted that eventually changed my life. My friend Dave suggested I contact his mother who was a professional career consultant. I do not know if Dave knows this today, but he helped save my life. Thank you Dave! So in December of 2001 I called Dave's mother Barbara Hill who changed my life.

Barbara showed me new hope that through some soul searching I would find my purpose in life. She pulled me out of my "life" rut that I had spent so many years decorating with fear, confusion, and greed. She is to this day a dear friend and mentor.

 I was standing at the crossroads of life facing a major decision to continue down the path of familiarity and misery or to break free from my comfort zone towards a more rewarding and fulfilling life?

I chose the latter and have not looked back since. Two weeks later my yellow lab Jake and I loaded up a U-Haul trailer and headed for Charlotte, NC. Even though I knew nobody in Charlotte and I was unemployed, I knew this would be the beginning of an incredible journey of self-discovery.

For the next eight months Barbara and I worked through her inspirational Kaleidoscope career exploration program. I walked away with a new set of values, a new footing for a better life, and a new design for living. My outlook on life changed as my insecurities were replaced by confidence, despair replaced by hope, and fear replaced by a foundation of faith. My new personal mission statement was:

To work with students and adults to help them incorporate their personal passions into their professional careers.

My seven-year plan/dream was to become an independent career counselor with a career exploration camp for adults in transition. There is nothing better than to escape into the mountainous terrain of God's country to reflect on self. I was on my way.

To get started towards that dream I entered the education field as an Eighth Grade Algebra Teacher and Coach of the girls' softball team at Quail Hollow Middle School.

During that process I could have just dropped off my resume with the robotic employee sitting at the Human Resources desk and waited for someone to call to offer me a job. That's what most people do in today's society. I decided to take a different approach called proactivity. I decided to visit every middle school in Monroe County, introduce myself to each principal and, express my desire to teach at their school, open position or not.

As unqualified as I seemed to any logical person, I received a call from the Principal at Quail Hollow Middle School that had a sudden teaching vacancy. Had I not visited that school on the day I did, I would have missed that opportunity. This goes to show that persistence and reliance upon the guiding hand of God truly pays off, time and time again.

What an incredible ride. It is amazing how much I learned from those little rascals, on and off the field. They tried my patience, yet filled my heart with love. They failed, then succeeded. Over ninety percent of my students worked hard to pass their state tests. The Lady Falcons Softball team led me to a memorable 9-1 season (plus we outscored our opposition by an average of 12 runs a game). I can only say thank you to those inspirational kids, the staff at Quail Hollow, and to Coach Tripp and Coach Paul for teaching me the "rules of the game!"

My new direction started to become more focused. And then the day came again when I stood at the crossroads of life facing yet another major decision. Stay at the middle school level or move closer to my dream of becoming a career counselor?

A few months prior to this decision, a close friend, Tracey, gave me a bookmark that read:

"Go confidently into the direction of your dreams. Live the life you always imagined." – Henry David Thoreau

That simple phrase became my new motto. After many conversations with my mentors, the decision to leave Charlotte and pursue a position in higher education as a career counselor was in motion.

I had a "Rob Lohman closeout" garage sale, packed my van with the necessities, donated the rest to Salvation Army, and Jake and I headed towards the Midwest. People thought I was nuts to quit a job without another job lined up, but I knew the decision was the right one because faith was guiding me. This approach worked before so why not try it again?

As I searched and searched for a career counseling position in the midwestern states I came across an opening for an Assistant Director at Indiana University in Bloomington. Within thirty minutes I contacted Arlene Hill at the Career Center to arrange an informational interview. She agreed. Two days later I was sitting in her office discussing the position. Arlene informed me that two more positions were opening up next week. Luck? Perfect timing? Who cares!

Two weeks later I passed their telephone interview (Interviewing HINT #1: By listening during the interview I picked up on several ladies interest in softball, so I ended the interview with my winning record as the Softball Coach at Quail Hollow).

Two weeks after that I passed their final onsite interview (Interviewing HINT #2: Two hours before my interview I dropped off two dozen Krispy Kreme donuts to the office staff).

Three weeks after that the Career Development Center at Indiana University in Bloomington hired me as a new Assistant Director. Amazing how things work out when you believe in your faith and add a little bit of persistence, listening, and donuts!

Whether I was teaching an eight-week career class to 170 juniors and seniors, counseling students at advising appointments, or critiquing resumes, I loved helping students. It's so cool when a student, who reminds me of me, stops by to say "Thank you for caring and helping me." That's the reward because it was surely not the pay, although the compensation package was quite attractive.

While working at IU, my passion for helping students strengthened. I wanted to impact their lives on a larger scale, but was not sure how. I wanted to share my experience, strength, and hope about the "real world" with college students to help them understand that college is a time to explore their interests, not plan their entire life.   Little did I know but the conception of The Momentum Journey was building inside of my soul.

Section 4 ..... Inspirations from Above

A new plan for my life began to unfold. In December 2003, I read "The Dream Giver" written by Bruce Wilkinson. The turn of each page drew me deeper and deeper into the modern-day parable of breaking free from the comfort-zone of life to pursue a Big Dream while overcoming fears, obstacles, and the pessimisms of society. I would recommend this inspirational read to anyone who lacks purpose and direction.

In January 2004, my friend Amy Brugh showed me an inspirational documentary about the different paths people follow to discover their true passions for life. Her enthusiasm for my newfound direction truly propelled me into action. Amy always says that "She is my number one fan." How could that not make a person feel great?

The little spark from "The Dream Giver" and from Amy grew into a passionate fire that no hurricane could extinguish. A purpose for my life and existence on Earth had finally revealed itself.

With all of the excitement whirling around in my hyperactive brain I began to pray for direction and clarity. I started bringing my notes to life with drawings on the bedroom walls of my apartment. Colors. Shapes. Flowcharts. Lists. Inspirations.

My roommates thought I was nuts. Not knowing where all of this was leading me, I experienced elation, confusion of my will versus His will, fear, faith, and an array of other emotions.

By the end of January a faint picture began to materialize consisting of three concepts:

1) visiting college campuses talking with students about their career struggles

2) developing for-credit internships that would create educational value, not paper-pushing skills, and

3) interviewing entrepreneurial minded people who were passionate about their career and willing to share their experience, strength, and hope with students around the nation.

The end result of these efforts would be to conduct motivational presentations at a variety of colleges and high schools across the country to inspire students to be entrepreneurial in their own career journey.

These concepts created a solid foundation for the direction of my newfound passions. Now I needed a name for this idea. So began another round of brainstorming on my bedroom walls.

~~The American Dream. The Self-Discovery Tour, The Passionate Quest, Passionate Explorations, It's All About You Journey, The Quest for Self, The Momentous Quest, The Destination, not The Journey~~….and so on.

After a few days of brainstorming the word momentum and the phrase "Life is journey, not a destination" stuck in my head.   Suddenly......The Momentum Journey was officially born.

Do you believe that everything happens for a reason? Or that IT is all part of God's plan? Or that failure presents a learning opportunity? I believe God puts people in my life to help with my own direction and my own character development. I do not question why certain things happen. I have learned that the real gift from any encounter may not occur for weeks or months, and more will be revealed as time goes on.

Great things come to those who follow the sunlight of the Spirit (whatever you consider your own Spirit to be.) Understanding that I am powerless over most things, except my own attitude, is very freeing. Try it sometime! It works. Also try to believe in yourself and believe in others.

I know that if I do the footwork, then the results will follow. Whatever we have is what we will have. I know that my faith has not brought me this far to drop me. I grow each day in the sunlight by living one day at a time. This is how my team and I will be living during our journey. As Joe Dirt says "Keep on Keepin' on!"

You have just read my story. It is now time to read the story of the momentum behind The Momentum Journey.

Reflections Page

At the end of each Part throughout this book, there will be a Reflections Page for you to contemplate your own journey in life.   Maybe the section you just read sparked some questions, thoughts, emotions, or other experiences in your career journey.   This part is all about YOU!

Part Two –
A New Path

"When one door closes another door opens; but we so often look so long and so regretfully upon the closed door, that we do not see the ones which open for us."
– Alexander Graham Bell, American inventor

Section 5 ..... The Momentum Begins

The Momentum Journey had been birthed! Now what? First step was to find inspirational people to interview for a series of documentaries. A co-worker at Indiana University, Jeremy Podany, had the February 2003 Issue of Black Enterprise Magazine sitting on his shelf with a catchy front cover (I forget the actual headings). This caught my attention, especially an article titled "Is Your Career Your Calling?" with a subtitle "Reverend and Former Basketball Star Paula McGee Explains The Difference Between What You Do and What You Are Meant To Be."
With each word in Paula's story I wanted to know more. I was engaged, curious, and inspired. McGee stated:

"I was a basketball player, and I was very good at it, but it wasn't my calling; it was only my career." She later stated *"...if you find your calling and pursue it, life will become an adventure."*

The word pursue caught my attention because so many people talk about dreams and never pursue them. Paula McGee realized her calling. Her calling became Paula McGee Ministries, a nonprofit organization dedicated to inspiring people "to recognize, accept, and fulfill their call to greatness."

On February 10th, 2004 I emailed Reverend McGee an invitation to participate in the documentary interviewing process.

Leaving the result of the email in God's hands, I focused on finding more people to contact for a potential interview.   Paula later became confirmed Interviewee #1. (Refer to Appendix I)

Where could I find more passionate people like Paula? Borders Bookstore of course. The next day I grabbed my coffee cup, pads of paper, colored pens, headphones, and started towards Borders for an afternoon of research. Ten hours, twenty magazines from a variety of industries, eight hundred pages, five cups of coffee, fifty pages of notes, and a half dozen hand cramps later, the initial list of passionate entrepreneurs was compiled. Up to this point in my life I had never been more inspired than I was at that moment. People have amazing stories to share. Now I had to see how willing they were to share them with The Momentum Journey.

Hours upon hours I spent tracking down the email addresses and phone numbers of potential interviewees. I would wake up at 5:00 a.m. to contact people on the east coast. I would make calls during my lunch breaks to contact people in the Midwest. Contact people on the west coast from 5:30 – 8:00 in the evening. Excitement was all around me.

After initial contacts were made I would send them an email with more details about The Momentum Journey's mission. I knew the email had to grab the recipient's attention so I spent a few days praying for direction.   The contextual foundation of The Momentum Journey surfaced. (Refer to Appendix II)

By March 8th, 2004 over thirty people agreed to share their story about their struggles, their sacrifices, and their journey along their search for passion. Below are a few of the first thirty confirmed interviewees:

Reverand Paula McGee
- Founder of Paula McGee Ministries

Hal O'Leary
- Founder of the National Sports Center for the Disabled

Laura Roberts
- CEO of Pantheon Chemicals

Chrissy Azzaro
- Founder of My-Tee

Brian Lee
- President of LegalZoom.com, Inc.

Sheila Dardashti
- Co-founder of Treesje Handbags

Lynda Weinman
- President of Lynda.com

Troy Jones
- President of EthnoImages, Inc.

Jennifer Roitman
- Mental Toughness Trainer of Head Games

Shell Herman
- CEO and Director of KidzArt

Jim Ford
- Franchisee of Woodcraft Supply Corporation

Ever heard of these people before? Probably not. They are the inspirations in your local communities. They are the heartbeat of America. They made life-changing sacrifices to pursue their passions in life. They love waking up every morning because they are participating in life, not "going to work" everyday.

The momentum was building much faster than I anticipated. Slightly unprepared, I began to realize that The Momentum Journey would become reality very soon. I needed to build a team. I needed transportation. I needed funding. I needed to ask for more direction from my mentors. I needed a plan.
Born and raised in Fort Wayne, IN I decided to start tapping into some of my Fort Wayne roots:

My cousin Jennifer Thompson created our original "standing at the crossroads of life" logo.

Toby Hatch with Indigo Printing started us with 500 business cards shaped like a little red license plate. Tom Hume of Hume and Communications in Bloomington, IN created our initial web site.

These people were part of the initial momentum behind The Momentum Journey. Thank you.

Section 6 ..... The Plan

The phrases "....No man can build a house until he first envisions a plan for it." and "Failing to plan *is* planning to fail." amplified inside my hyperactive brain.

Therefore I spent the next ten days intensely studying the ingredients of successful organizations around the country. Through a compilation of those ingredients, input from my mentors, prayer and meditation, and the willingness to succeed, I managed to incorporate The Momentum Journey, Inc. as a nonprofit organization in the State of Colorado on March 22nd, 2004.

Why Colorado? Because that is where I eventually desired to plant roots. The momentum continued to build.

The next step involved finding an enthusiastic team. But how? Who? Where? As with any new idea I knew spiritual guidance was essential. Quiet times of meditation a must. After a few hours I began writing down the names of everyone I knew. Four hundred eighty names later the list ended. This turned out to be more like a gratitude list. A list full of good and bad memories. A list about my life. Surely wasn't expecting that when I started the "potential team" list. As I pondered the list I realized that all of those people influenced my life in some way. Those people helped me get to where I was in my life at that exact moment. God works in mysterious ways.

The list shortened and shortened and shortened.......

Finally I decided to start contacting a few people about my incredibly inspirational journey ahead. Would anyone join me? The news was received enthusiastically by most. Then the day arrived when Journeyer #1 was revealed. It happened in the Starbuck's at Kirkwood and Indiana Avenue in Bloomington, IN.

A few days prior to April 17th, 2004 (exactly one year ago as I wrote this page) I contacted a student who attended a course I taught the semester before. I remembered her spunky personality, her popularity among her peers, and her passion to enjoy life. After a few cups of coffee the facts were on the table. We

discussed the rewards, the risks, and everything else that surfaced during our energized conversation. Melanie Gideon became Journeyer #1.

Mel loved the idea so much that we met again a few days later with her friend Aric Geesaman. We again discussed the risks involved, but we all knew the risks were minimal compared to the life experience and the impact of our future results. Aric became Journeyer #2.

I asked both to discuss their post-college decision with their parents. Whatever happened during those talks lead to Melanie and Aric's commitment to officially join The Momentum Journey team. I was so fired up with enthusiasm! Now all we needed was funding and an RV.

I developed an action plan covering the next few months. Over the next few weeks we (I can now say we because it was not just me anymore) agreed on the individual roles each would play on the team.

Melanie…media and public relations.

Aric……marketing and campus relations.

Me…..everything else.

We spent the next few months combining our talents to establish a nationwide marketing plan. Within specific cities close to our sixty-five scheduled interviewees we researched contact information of newspapers, radio stations, business and trade magazines, college career development centers, high school principals, special events, and professional / college sporting events. Melanie and Aric did an incredible job during this process.   Anticipated launch date of Phase I was scheduled for August 25th, 2004. Did we meet that date? Time would tell.

Now we needed funding and an RV.   Without funds….no RV, so funding took priority. Melanie and Aric got busy creating a spreadsheet of more than 450 names of alumni from my fraternity. We would then send each alumnus clever marketing postcards to hopefully start raising funds. I started researching companies through a series of web sites like Hoovers.com, google.com, entrepreneur.com and so on. I compiled a list of 250 companies that met the following criteria: 1)   supported educational programming, 2) marketed to students, 3) had disposable income, and 4) were entrepreneurially minded.

Upon completion of our lists we mailed letters and postcards to the masses. The content described The

Momentum Journey's mission and listed the benefits of their potential involvement. The results were in God's hands. Our focus was to create awareness. We didn't really expect tons of cash to arrive in my mailbox. What was the response? Time would tell.

The next few weeks involved contacting each of the 250 companies through email and/or telephone. It is known in the marketing industry that a person will receive a hundred "nos" before they receive a "yes". How did we do? We received two "maybes." Better than a no. I quickly realized that mass mailings were not the way to proceed.

We still only had the funds in my personal account. How about a local fundraiser? Of course. Three weeks later I managed to put together The Momentum Journey's first Bowlarama Fundraiser on July 24th, 2004. Various local businesses donated items for door prizes and a silent auction. The turnout was way below my realistic expectations, but we did manage to make a few dollars. As tough as it was I had to remember that if I do the footwork, then God will provide. Back to the drawing board.

Since purchasing an RV was out of the question, I thought we would try to get one donated. I compiled a list of RV manufacturers across the country, contacted the gatekeeper for the CEO, and mailed out marketing packages to over 15 manufacturers. I learned from the poor results we had from the 250 companies we tried to contact earlier that sending out some "tester" packages to the RV manufacturers would be a wise idea. Slight interest from one manufacturer out of South Bend, IN gave us hope. That fell through but opened another door to another innovative idea.

Go door to door to RV dealers. The result? You guessed it…time would tell.

Through the use an internet mapping site, I mapped out and contacted RV dealers within a 30 mile radius of Indianapolis. Melanie and I started with the largest dealer in the area. We expected they would like our concept of advertising their dealership on the back of a donated RV that would travel over thirty thousand miles within two years. Mel and I spent about forty minutes in amazement as we toured incredibly spacious RVs ranging from a twenty-two foot $40K to a thirty-eight foot $295K motorhome.

After touring the RVs we finally heard our names over the speakers to begin our scheduled meeting with the owner of the RV lot. Mel and I were ready to pitch our idea and drive away in a new RV. Yeah right! Rejection number one, followed by rejection number two, number three, and so on. At least we tried!

Section 7 ….. The "RV" Experience

On August 5th, 2004 I came across the following ad in The Herald-Times:

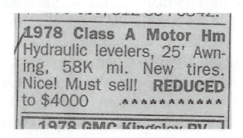

1978 Class A Motor Hm Hydraulic levelers, 25' Awning, 58K mi. New tires. Nice! Must sell! **REDUCED** to $4000 ★★★★★★★★★★★★

1978 GMC Kingsley RV

Knowing diddly squat about cars, much less Recreational Vehicles, I contacted my friend Josh to come along for the potential RV purchase ride. As we rolled over the final approach hill we saw the massive 35 foot long, off-white 1978 Holiday Rambler. While pulling into the driveway out of the house came Tony, a 5'5" intriguing character who was ready and willing to sell. (We found out on September 4th, 2004 why.)

In all of the excitement Josh, Tony, and I climbed into the living room of the RV for the grand tour. Immediately I shot out of the RV due to a large swarm of wasps hovering over the front AC unit. Tony quickly yelled inside for his lovely wife to bring some wasp spray. After Tony "hot shotted" the wasps and death came upon them, we continued the tour.

From the rear was a full bathroom, then a "bedroom", full kitchen with new cabinets and hardwood floors, full-size living room with new carpet and probably the ugliest couch you had ever seen, and finally the "cockpit" consisting of numerous gadgets and controls. Tony fired up The 1978 Rambler and off we went. The power behind the Dodge 440 Magnum engine was quite impressive and invoked a bit of fear.

Tony cranked some AC/DC that bellowed in the RV from front to back. We quickly discovered that Tony might have had a few too many cocktails prior to our arrival so we encouraged him to turn around and head home. With no problem at all Tony turned the thirty-five foot RV around on a tiny country road.

Once stationary again, Josh determined that the engine, tires (all ten of them) and few other essentials were in good enough shape for a mere $3,500.00. The week prior Tony wanted $5,300. His current classified ad was for $4,000. I offered $3,000 cash, he countered at $3,700, and I finally counted out thirty-five $100 bills to become the new owner of The Rambler!   With title in hand I drove home in The Momentum Journey's primary mode of transportation.

I contacted Melanie and Aric to inform them of their future living accommodations. They were shocked at the age of The Rambler, but I assured them of safe travel.   They then realized that our targeted launch date of August 25th was now possible.

Due to The Ramblers bumper-to-bumper length I parked it in the middle school parking lot across the street from my apartment, contacted the local police so my illegally parked RV would not get towed, moved in over the next few days, then transitioned it to Josh's side yard for a week to get The Rambler ready for the upcoming nationwide inspirational journey.

Approaching local paint and hardware stores to try and score some free painting supplies sounded like a great idea.   The manager of the Bloomington, IN Lowe's store agreed to donate two gallons of quite red paint, rollers, tape, brushes and a few other items. Amazing how some off-the-wall ideas actually materialize!

The following weekend I sanded down the entire RV with a surface area of 1,000 square feet. My incredibly artistic cousin Jennifer and her husband Pat drove down from Indianapolis to complete the transition of The Rambler to Big Red. Six hours later, Big Red was finished and looked better than ever. Onlookers would drive by and ask if Big Red was Indiana University's new Party Bus. I quickly smashed that concept but it was great to know that Big Red would not go unnoticed. This was an awesome day. Big Red shined with confidence.

About a month prior I contacted Young Money Magazine about The Momentum Journey's upcoming launch date. A few hours after Big Red acquired a new look, a Young Money reporter called.   Forty-five minutes later we concluded the exciting interview. That kicked up the momentum one more notch.

The next day I decided to take Big Red for a quick spin. The one thing I forgot was that you just cannot turn around a thirty-five foot vehicle wherever you want. I started heading to where I thought I could find a clearing to turn around.   To my dismay I had to continue down three miles of narrowing, winding roads with low lying branches. All I heard was thump, crack, screech, and a few other sounds. I had no choice but to proceed ahead at a turtles pace. I finally found a place large enough to accommodate my needs. All I can say is that Big Red came through unscathed. Whew!

The day came to depart from Bloomington towards Fort Wayne, Indiana to rendezvous with Melanie and Aric. Would Big Red make it to Fort Wayne?

Section 8 ….. The Fort Wayne, IN Experience

OF COURSE! Three hours later Big Red safely arrived at Exit 102 in Fort Wayne, Indiana. My grandmother, a.k.a. Gammy, happened to be out of town for a few weeks so her driveway became Big Red's new home. Melanie and Aric were to arrive in a few days. Keep in mind they have never laid eyes upon the beauty of Big Red. Were they in for a surprise.

The next couple of days were spent gathering materials to construct bed frames and extra storage for the bedroom. Since my Uncle Dave happened to be a gadget guy, he offered his garage to be the designated "construction zone." Power tools hummed nonstop. Hammers pounded nail after nail. Within thirty-six hours the construction of two (one for each side of the bedroom) six-foot by four-foot by three-foot bed frames with extra storage were completed. Installation would commence in a few days.

Mel and Aric arrived from Michigan on August 14th, just eleven days before the scheduled launch date of Phase I of The Momentum Journey. I wish I would have filmed their expressions when they viewed Big Red for the first time. It was priceless.

The next week we worked diligently cleaning Big Red from top to bottom. This was quite a chore. Mel hated the wood paneling in the living room, so we painted it off-white for three reasons: 1) Mel, 2) to have better light balancing for filming interviews inside the RV, and 3) so visitors could sign the inside walls of Big Red.

On August 22nd a huge thunderstorm tore through Fort Wayne. Did Big Red's roof withstand the rain? Nope. I cautiously entered the living room to find what I hoped not to find...two roof leaks. Dang! Better to find out now than later. I believe this was a sign, so I decided to take Big Red in for immediate roof inspection, a tune-up, and a few other minor repairs.

Kelley Chevrolet in Fort Wayne was the only dealership that could work on a 1978 Holiday Rambler. So on the morning of August 23rd I drove Big Red to her first scheduled doctors appointment for her first physical. On the way I stopped to fill up at a gas station large enough to accommodate a twelve foot tall RV. I guess she was nervous like a child going to the doctor for the first time because forty feet later Big Red died. That's right. Smack dab in the middle of rush hour traffic on Spy Run. I could see the dealership two blocks away. Two blocks! What now?

I called my insurance company to get a tow. They said it would be about an hour before a tow truck would arrive. Kelley Chevrolet did not have a truck big enough to tow Big Red, so I sat and sat and sat.... Horns were honking. People were yelling. Finally a police officer arrived to lend assistance. He gave me ten flares to use until the tow truck arrived. Little did he know we would need those flares again real soon.

The tow truck finally arrived. The driver, John, suggested I try firing up the engine again. Wow! She started immediately. John followed me to Big Red's appointment and wished me luck. Little did I know but Big Red was much more ill than anticipated. Diagnosis: new starter, generator needed to be rewired, carburetor needed work, roof leaks easily repairable, tune-up would be costly, and a few other minor symptoms. Timeframe...ten days.

This obviously delayed our anticipated launch date of August 25th. Mel, Aric, and I spent the next ten days canceling the scheduled interviews with our Colorado interviewees. The dealership allowed us to visit Big Red in the evenings to finish preparing the interior for our next scheduled launch date of September 4th. Disappointed? Yes, but the team seemed alright with the delay. Spirits were optimistic. Time was on our side.

On September 1st, Melanie and Aric surprised me with a "to scale" map of the United States painted on the side of Big Red.   I was completely floored by their efforts. This meant so much to me that I actually got a bit teary eyed. Now we could track our route across the country. Big Red looked better than ever.

The rest of the night involved disassembling the bed frames because they would not fit through the hallway door leading to the bedroom. Oops. Guess I didn't consider that. No problem. Two hours later the frames were installed, all of Mel and Aric's stuff was loaded inside the immaculately cleaned RV, and it was ready for travel. Big Red was released the next day and parked infront of the September 4th launch location.

Reflections Page

Part Three –
Launch Day - September 4th, 2004

"The longer I live, the more I realize the impact of attitude on life. Attitude, to me, is more important than the past, than education, than money, than circumstances, than failures, than successes, than what other people think or say or do. It is more important than appearance, giftedness or skill. It will make or break a company...a church...a home. The remarkable thing is we have a choice every day regarding the attitude we will embrace for that day. We cannot change our past...we cannot change the fact that people will act in a certain way. We cannot change the inevitable. The one thing we can do is play on the one string we have, and that is our attitude. I am convinced that life is 10% what happens to me and 90% how I react to it. And so it is with you...we are in charge of our attitudes." —Charles Swindoll

Section 9 ….. Fill 'er up please?

Six in the morning wake up call. Big Red's looking good. Sun shining. No clouds. Full tank of gas. Eager to hit the road. Melanie and Aric arrived at the launch location at 8:15 a.m. Aric's grandparents arrived at 8:45. My Uncle Dave, Aunt Andrea (A.O.), and cousins Sara (Bear) and Andrew (Shorty) joined us in their front yard for the send-off ceremony. Big Red was loaded and ready to head to California.
At 9:13 a.m. Mel, Aric, Jake, and I said our good-byes to our family and stepped aboard our new home for the next few months. At 9:14 I said a quick prayer to our Mighty protector. At 9:15 the ignition key was inserted and…………VROOOOOM, VROOOM…..Big Red started right up. Whew!

Aric enthusiastically stated "The door is locked. Let The Momentum Journey begin!"
I replied with a "Yahooooo!"
Mel gave Jake a high-five.

The Momentum Journey officially started with a successful launch down Woodstream Lane in Fort Wayne, IN. About three hundred yards into our initial leg we had to stop our momentum. Was it engine trouble? A flat tire? Electrical trouble? No, no, and another no. It was my Aunt Sally walking down the street so we stopped to say goodbye. Now we were officially on our way.

With cameras rolling inside the RV, our excitement through the roof, and open road ahead we pointed south towards Indianapolis. While approaching Indy we encountered a detour off of I-69 due to construction. In case you didn't know, Big Red only accomplished six m.p.g. This would be our largest expense during the journey. We decided to take this opportunity to fill up. Smooth sailing so far! Fill up complete. All aboard. Key in ignition. Turning key in ignition and......nothing. Nothing happened at all. Not even a cough from Big Red. What was happening? It was.......**BREAKDOWN #1**

Mel: "We are having many of several minor difficulties"

Aric: "We lost our momentum for a short period of time."

Me: "It's all about getting to know her [Big Red]"

The mechanic at the Kelly Chevrolet mentioned we may have trouble with "hot starts." We just learned what he meant. After about twenty minutes of cooldown time, I poured a few drops of gasoline directly into the carburetor, sealed the engine cover, prayed, and then Aric yells "Moment of truth...come on baby. No whammys." Big Red started immediately. Whew! (A common theme in this book).

Section 10 ….. Trouble on I-70

Now that we were mobile again, Aric took over the
cockpit to begin his first experience behind the wheel
of Big Red. About sixty miles later we encountered a
massive traffic jam on I-70 near Cloverdale. Traffic
stretched for fifteen miles. While idling, Big Red
decided to shut down and die. She wouldn't start
again. It was…..**BREAKDOWN #2.**

Mel: "We died again. This won't be the last time."

Aric and I jumped out, headed to the rear of Big Red,
and managed to push her onto the shoulder while Mel
steered us within six inches from the guardrail. You
should have seen Aric and I pushing this massive RV.
Once the momentum picked up Aric jumped back into
the RV and began filming me pushing Big Red down
the highway. People were cheering us on. It was a
classic moment of teamwork in action.

Aric: "We died.
We had to push it off the side of the road."
Mel: "Well, the power steering is out, so it was tough
trying to not hit the guardrail."

We ended up sitting in traffic for the next hour. Mel,
Aric, and I had the attitude of making the most of
every moment. Here was a chance to practice that
attitude. Mel and Aric ran off to play in the woods
with Jake. I observed other inconvenienced travelers.
Some were irate. Some snoozing. A trucker playing
with his dog caught my eye and I felt drawn to strike

up a conversation with him. I told him of our journey and asked for an interview. This trucker became Interviewee #1 for The Momentum Journey. Jean and I sat upon the guardrail next to Big Red and talked for about fifteen minutes.

Enjoy Jean Lawrence's story.

Where are you and your family heading?
Heading towards Terre Haute.

How did you get started? What are you doing right now?
My wife Barbara and I own our own trucking company called Just Cruzin' Enterprises – a one truck wonder from Sunrise Beach, Missouri.
Started driving for a different outfit, then we moved to Missouri twelve years ago from Chicago. Work was more difficult to find in Missouri than we were used to making, so I started driving trucks and my wife joined me (said while smiling at Barbara) shortly thereafter.
After working for a few different companies we bought our own truck and decided to go independent.

What do you like about it?
I like the freedom about it. We can call our shots as far as where we want to go. My family's pretty spread about the country so we can stop and visit people as the mood strikes. When we visit people we don't get a second chance to stay long enough to make 'em glad to see us twice. So it works out pretty well.
Lately we have been doing a lot of stuff in Florida hauling hurricane relief stuff down to Miami. We may go there

again depending on what happens with this hurricane [Frances]. We just take it as it goes.

Did you have any challenges getting stuff to Florida? Wasn't there a holding area?
We got there after the holding area. They were meeting people and bringing them in as needed. We were out of Florida at that time.
My sister and brother-in-law were vacationing in Florida near the Siesta Keys and we were delivering in their area. They evacuated their hotel and they were trying to get a flight out so we ended up giving them a ride to Mobile, Alabama.
It's kind of interesting.

We're making this documentary to talk to high school and college students about career decisions or struggles. Any advice?
Stay in school. I am still taking some time off. There's plenty of time to go make some money.
There are a lot of college degrees out there…driving a truck or working in an office. Just matters on what you want to do. So, stay in school.

What I learned in the brief time is that people have a story to tell and are willing to share that story if asked. Incorporate this concept in your daily life. Start asking people around you about their life. Have you known someone for a long time but really don't know them? I know I do and now I ask them to share their story with me. And then I sit……..and listen.
Traffic started moving again so we concluded the interview and went our separate ways.

Section 11 ….. How did you miss that?

Big Red started right up to head in a westward direction towards California. We were so glad to be mobile again.   About twenty miles later we were cruising about sixty m.p.h. over a blind hill on the interstate when just over the crest was another accident. This time we almost totaled Big Red. Aric quickly swerved, just missing the right rear corner of a stopped eighteen wheeler and somehow managed to squeeze us between the semi and the guardrail.   An ultra frightening experience. Everything that was loose in the RV came crashing forward upon Jake, Mel, and me.   Luckily nobody was injured.   Our Protector definitely had His hand upon us.

Once our momentum finally stopped we said a quick prayer and removed all of the upfront clutter. While idling Big Red stalled again.   We couldn't run the generator because the exhaust seemed to be ventilating back into the RV and we were almost completely out of gas. We sat and sat and sat for another thirty minutes. It was…**BREAKDOWN #3.**

Section 12 ….. Stop sign stall

Traffic began moving again.   Big Red fired up immediately. We decided to relieve Aric of his driving duties! Next stop….gas station. Nineteen miles later the Casey, IL exit appeared.

While approaching the off-ramp stop sign I wanted to roll through to avoid a stall, but the cross-traffic was horrendous and.............we stalled. Big Red's engine was hot and tired. She wouldn't turn over. Tank empty. We were stuck just two hundred yards from the gas station across the interstate. It was.... **BREAKDOWN #4.**

Section 13 ….. Popcorn anyone?

Aric and Mel had had enough, so they ventured over to the gas station to relax and cool off. We had been on the road for eight hours and only traveled two hundred seventy miles. Jake and I stayed with Big Red, called roadside assistance, unfolded my camping chair, and sat outside the RV waiting for the tow truck. Onlookers slowed to offer assistance but there was nothing they could do for our sick motorhome. I decided to try starting Big Red one last time. With key in the ignition I gave it one crank and.........VROOOOOM. Big Red's little engine mustered enough energy to make it over the bridge and suddenly die as I approached the closest gas pump. WHEW!
I was hot, hungry, and tired. We all sat inside for twenty minutes to regroup. What exciting thing could happen next?
Some locals at the gas station mentioned the Annual Casey Popcorn Festival was happening all day. Hmmmmm? A popcorn festival? Why not? Mel, Aric,

and I decided to attend the festival to let Big Red rest a while, then we would drive all night in cooler temperatures. We also decided to head towards Texas to stay at my folks place for a few days and get the RV looked at again. This plan made the most sense. It also eased our minds. Guess what? Big Red died again on the way to the festival.

A nice man approached the driver's window and said:

"Do ya wunna use my cellar phone? Come on in.?" It was....**BREAKDOWN #5.**

With a couple of cranks Big Red fired back up.   We parked by the softball fields and headed into the most interesting Popcorn Festival filled with zebras, camels, an untalented guy trying to be Michael Jackson, chocolate covered bananas, cotton candy, antiques, and many other unmentionable sights.   Our visit to the Casey Popcorn Festival allowed each of us the opportunity to forget our problems of the day.   It provided an outlet for relaxation. It probably saved us from complete exhaustion.

We hit the road again towards St. Louis to meet up with some of Mel's friends. Do you think our troubles were over?   Would Big Red make it another one hundred thirty seven miles?

Reflections Page

Part Four –
Breakdown at Exit 63

"I am not afraid of storms for I am learning how to sail my ship". – *Louisa May Alcott*

"When you get into a tight place and everything goes against you, till it seems as though you could not hang on a minute longer, never give up then, for that is just the place and time that the tide will turn."

– *Harriet Beecher Stowe*

Do you know that feeling you get when the power steering goes out in your car? No? Well imagine driving a thirty-five foot RV traveling 65 m.p.h. approaching a curve on Interstate 70 and suddenly the engine makes a POP, then a BANG, then a HISSSS, then starts to SMOKE, and finally the power steering quits. That's exactly what happened to Big Red while approaching Exit 63 in Vandalia, IL. It was..........**BREAKDOWN #6.**

Aric safely steered Big Red clear of all guardrails and bridges. Slowly we came to a halt upon the right shoulder just past Exit 63. Without thinking, Aric grabbed the fire extinguisher and I lifted the engine cover for inspiration (oops, I meant inspection). We realized our lack of planning and the potential danger of an engine fire, so we quickly vacated the RV. To protect Big Red we lit some flares (remember the ones that were donated from the cop in Fort Wayne?), called the insurance company, the state police, and headed to higher ground. Upon our approach to the Chuckwagon restaurant atop the hill, I noticed a beautiful yellow halo in the distance. For a reason to be revealed later, the halo thought vanished.

As we slowly gathered our wits, Aric and Mel asked how I was doing. I believe I responded with "As strange as it sounds, I am OK with this. It is definitely out of my control and I know it is all part of God's greater plan." I congratulated Aric on his superb driving. God's hand saved us once again as nobody was physically injured.

About forty-five minutes later Lynn with McDowell's Towing Service arrived. You should have seen the size of McDowell's huge red rig. I believe it was Big Red's long lost brother.

Aric and Mel rode shotgun in McDowell's rig. I rode shotgun with the Sheriff. Jake had to ride in the RV....all alone. I wondered what confusing thoughts were in Jake's mind during this interesting event?

We safely arrived at McDowell's garage, unhooked Big Red, and gathered a couple of days worth of belongings. Lynn made two trips to get us to our hotel. Remember that yellow halo above the Chuckwagon? It turned out to be the Days Inn in Vandalia, IL, just one mile from Big Red's last stand. The hotel receptionist turned out to be Lynn's nephew. We called him Happy Tim. Now we could relax.

We settled in our spacious hotel room, called family, and went to bed, grateful to be alive. God held our hand today. I knew He was working inside and through me. Aric and Mel felt the same way. Bedtime.

Since it was Labor Day Weekend we would have to wait for three days for a diagnosis of Big Red's condition. Now begins the next segment of our journey.

Section 14.... Day 1 – Abe Lincoln?

What do you do in a town in the middle of nowhere not knowing a single soul? Go see a movie? Nope because there was only one movie playing one day a week (Wednesday) and it was The Princess Diaries. That idea took care of itself. Learn about Vandalia, IL? This idea became the focus of the morning. Here is what we learned about Vandalia, IL....

1.   First capitol of Illinois.
2.   Abe Lincoln used to practice law here.
3.   Downtown had a Lincoln Memorial building.
4.   There was a Wal-Mart.

Instead of dwelling on the negatives, we knew we had to make the most of the situation. As a cost savings decision, we walked to the nearest grocery store to stock up on food and drinks. Mel managed to secure a ride back to the hotel from a kind local couple. We were able to share our exciting journey with them. Exciting? Definitely. We could not have written a script as perfect as the one thus far before we left Fort Wayne, Indiana a mere thirty-six hours prior.

Section 15.... Day 2 – Wally-World

Happy Tim greeted us in the morning with a grin and a "Please let me know what I can do to make your stay at the Days Inn a pleasant one". Passing by Happy Tim, the three of us enjoyed a scrumptious continental breakfast, read the newspaper, made some phone calls to loved ones, and headed back to the room for some rest and relaxation.

What's the best thing to do when you need to kill a few hours? Head to Wal-Mart of course. Mel happened to meet a woman in the Days Inn lobby and discussed with her our mission of the day...... get to Wal-Mart. This energetic woman actually called up her daughter to help us accomplish our mission. How awesome was this? We are in a place where we don't know a soul and local residents are reaching out their hands to help us through this transitional period. Humanity had been restored!

Thirty minutes later a black Durango pulls up, the passenger window is lowered, and sitting in the driver's seat is this kind woman's daughter Alison.

Once at Wally-World, we all separated for an hour to accommodate our individual needs. I proceeded to the Customer Service counter to chat with a manager about a gift card donation to help us during our stay in Vandalia. Attempt #1 failed, but persistence is the name of the game. On the sixth day a $25.00 gift card surfaced. Thanks Wal-Mart.

I proceeded to the RV section noticing an elderly couple in the septic area. I decided to strike up a conversation. During our chat I learned about the incredible historical places they journeyed to in their functioning RV. Sam and Wendy seemed enamored with each other. You could tell that love was their common bond. As we discussed our plight, they sympathized and we parted ways. It is so special to converse with people around the country and just listen to their story. People will share if they are asked.

Our hour ended. We rendezvoused outside the exit of Wal-Mart to enjoy our snacks and swap stories. I set up the video camera to film our strategy session for the next step of the day. After all, we did accomplish our mission of getting to Wal-Mart. Now we had to get back to the hotel.

We managed to track down another couple, Steve and Carol, who generously transported us to McDowell's to visit Big Red. Aric and I played some football. Mel read a book and slept. The time came for Alison to pick us up and head back to the Days Inn.

Pizza for dinner. Movie for entertainment.

Section 16.... Day 3 - Silence

Not much to report. Sat by the pool. Jotted down contingency plans. Sort of a free day for everyone.

Section 17.... Day 4 - The $6,000.00 phone call

The natives were getting restless so we decided to do some filming in downtown Vandalia. We needed a car. Whalla! I was conversing with Happy Tim in the morning and a young man overheard our conversation about me trying to find some friends of mine in the area. With a quick dial of seven numbers the tall slender stranger called a mystery person. This person happened to be his father, Ed, who just happened to be the owner of the Days Inn and who just happened to know my friends of Bill W.

Remember that yellow halo I saw the night Big Red broke down? I realized that God was directing us to the Days Inn for safe shelter and to be placed in the hands of Ed. Ed became a saving grace. Because of our common bond of friends Ed loaned us his conversion van so we could get around town with no trouble. It was that moment that I strongly believed that by being a trustworthy person and practicing trustworthy principles, people will sense a person's trustworthiness.

In addition, Ed opted to ride his scooter to and from work so we could utilize his van. Thank you Ed for believing in us! And thank you for introducing us to your lovely family.

Note to the reader: We would recommend stopping by to see Ed and his staff at the Days Inn at Exit 63 in Vandalia, IL. Let them know The Momentum Journey sent you. They'll love that.

Back to the story. Now that we had wheels.....first stop.....the Lincoln Memorial. CLOSED! Next stop.....local library. OPEN. Finally a chance to plug into the world wide web. High speed at that! Emails galore. Some time to forget about our plight, so I thought. After checking my bank account online I realized I had made a deposit into the wrong account on the day we launched Big Red. OOPS! Therefore, in big red (no pun intended) numbers my statement read -$458.00. It gets worse. There was not a branch for my bank within a two hundred fifty mile radius.

Thankfully I contacted my personal banker, Lisa B., and she patched up my mistake. So far, lots of positives in day four in Vandalia.

A few minutes later my cell phone rings. It's McDowell's with an update. The voice on the other end suggested I sit down before she breaks the news. Engine breakdown. Engine locked up beyond repair. $1,500 to tear engine apart to inspect. If mechanical then insurance covers repairs. If not, then $6,000 to replace. Six-thousand dollars!!!!!! Crap. Crap. More crap. I hit my knees and prayed for an answer. Whatever the answer was to be it would be, but I needed one fast.

After lamenting in my morass of self-pity consisting of my pride and my ego, I headed into the library to grab Aric and Mel. As we sat in Ed's conversion van I asked Aric to turn on the camcorder for a final debriefing. I informed the team that the physical momentum of The Momentum Journey was dead. Not over, but dead for now. As a team we decided that disassembling the team was the only option.

We shared our honest thoughts on tape.

We prayed for direction.

We went about our day.

We visited the local Depot restaurant and began to prepare for Plan B.

Are you asking yourself why I keep plugging on? I had to question that myself. But I believed in my heart of hearts that The Momentum Journey was my calling in life. To this calling I would dedicate my waking moments forthcoming.

<<<<<<<<<<<<<<<<<<<<<<<<<>>>>>>>>>>>>>>>>>>>>>>>>>

Section 18.... Day 5 : 27 – 17 =?

Trying to find a U-Haul for a one-way trip from Vandalia, IL to Fort Wayne, IN was as difficult as you might have thought. I'll say that nothing comes easy for The Momentum Journey team. Mel spent hours on the phone locating a U-Haul dealer with a truck small enough to haul their belongings. Finally, Mel found a place just around the corner. What should have taken about twenty minutes to reserve the truck ended in a ninety minute nightmare. The fella renting us the truck had a dinosaur computer with an inch of dust on the top. The printer forgot what the word print meant. I had yet another chance to practice patience, love, and tolerance. In the faint background I heard the humm of a printer. Sweetness! Yeah a contract, with a slight glitch of course. The U-Haul truck was thirty-five miles away in Effingham, IL.

Ed let us use his van that evening to pick up the ten foot truck Mel reserved. Upon arrival at the truck depot we were presented the keys to a twenty-seven foot U-Haul, seventeen feet longer than the one we reserved. Seventeen feet! The story gets better.

The only other truck available was a ten foot truck with a bad starter. Figures. If we wanted to wait for an hour they would install a new starter. After a team huddle we agreed to their solution. Hunger struck us at once so we headed to Friday's for lunner (that's sort of like brunch, but the middle of lunch and dinner). Finally we arrived back in Vandalia with a working U-Haul. Bedtime.

<<<<<<<<<<<<<<<<<<<<<<<<<<>>>>>>>>>>>>>>>>>>>>>>>>

Section 19.... Day 6 – And then there were two

Definitely not a day any of us wanted to accept. You could feel the disappointment in the air. Melanie and Aric sacrificed so much to help me begin my dream of The Momentum Journey. They will always hold a special place in my heart of hearts. I would recommend them to any employer fortunate enough to hire them.

We started the day with a prayer followed by silence. Mel and Aric loaded up the U-Haul. I remember Aric stating "I feel like I am heading home with my tail between my legs, but I know everything happens for a reason. I am just scared."

We said our "see you again soons" (not goodbyes because we knew we would meet again). Jake and I gave them a blessed send-off. With the camera rolling, the mighty U-Haul vanished into the horizon. Aric and Mel were off to start their new chapters in life.

I spent the next couple of hours reflecting on the week. Despite the major setbacks, there were numerous tiny successes. Feelings of gratitude to be alive consumed me. I had become a doer and not just a dreamer. The fact that The Momentum Journey had come so far in just a short period of time could not have been accomplished if it was not meant to be.

The afternoon was spent in Ed's office determining what to do with Big Red. Ed offered to help me sell Big Red locally. He offered to store Big Red on the side parking lot of the Days Inn. We created a classified ad for the local newspaper using both of our names for contact information. I believe we even went to get a milkshake together later that day.

You have to be asking yourself the question "Why would a man like Ed help out a complete stranger the way he did?" The answer is simple...because Ed is human. Humanity oozed from the very soil where Vandalia was founded. There are people like Ed all around you, only if you are open to accept this train of thought.

<<<<<<<<<<<<<<<<<<<<>>>>>>>>>>>>>>>>>>>>>

Section 20.... Day 7 – Visions from a rear view mirror

8:00 a.m.
Took a Greyhound Bus from Vandalia to St. Louis
11:00 a.m.
Took a shuttle from Greyhound Bus station to St. Louis Airport
12:00 p.m.
Rental car to drive to Dallas/Fort Worth Airport
1:30 p.m.
Arrived back at the Days Inn in Vandalia
2:00 – 6:00 p.m.
Emptied Big Red and packed rental car
6:30 p.m.
Jake and I left the Days Inn in Vandalia, IL. Big Red would never be seen again, except in my dreams.
6:32 p.m.
Rental car broke down...just kidding. Jake and I entered I-70 from the Exit 63 onramp. Vandalia faded away in the rearview mirror.

Reflections Page

Part Five –
What's next for MOJO?

"Whatever you do, you need courage. Whatever course you decide upon, there is always someone to tell you you are wrong. There are always difficulties arising which tempt you to believe that your critics are right. To map out a course of action and follow it to the end, requires some of the same courage which a soldier needs. Peace has it victories, but it takes brave men to win them." – *Ralph Waldo Emerson*

The physical momentum of The Momentum Journey officially stopped in Vandalia, IL, but the spirit and vision lives on. I am dedicated to see the completion of my mission to inspire a nation of confused students and adults to be passionate about their life through exploring as many options as possible.   This is my calling!

Since the breakdown in Vandalia many exciting doors have opened for The Momentum Journey, so please visit www.themomentumjourney.org to check our progress since September 11th, 2004

Many passionate entrepreneurs are contacting The Momentum Journey to share their story in the hopes of inspiring students to explore as many avenues as possible in their pursuit for passion.   All of these stories will be posted on The Momentum Journey web site. Some stories will be shared in future inspirational books and some will be used during motivational presentations at college campuses across the nation.

I would like to thank you for purchasing *The Momentum Journey : Breakdown at Exit 63*. Your support will help us reach our $85,000.00 financial goal to re-launch the physical portion of The Momentum Journey by September 4th, 2005 (Big Red's Anniversary).

With the 2005-2006 academic year approaching, The Momentum Journey is busy scheduling motivational presentations about "Careers, Passion, and Entrepreneurialism" on high school and college campuses across the country. For more information, please email campusvisit@themomentumjourney.org.

The Momentum Journey is continually seeking investors that are excited about our educational programs. This is an incredible investment opportunity to not only receive a projected fifty percent return, but a chance to help inspire students to achieve their dreams. For more information, please send an email to invest@themomentumjourney.org.

If you would like to further support The Momentum Journey, then please visit our sponsorship section in Appendix III in this book or visit our web site. Online contributions may be made through the web site or mailed to:

> The Momentum Journey, Inc.
> P.O. Box 4238
> Edwards, CO 81632
> (970) 331-4469

*The above mailing address is subject to change, so please refer to the web site for updated information.

Thank you again for believing in The Momentum Journey.

Gratefully,

Rob "The MOJO Man" Lohman

Part Six –
Meet the Passionates!

"What would you attempt to do if you could not fail?"

- unknown

The following chapters are the stories of some of the original interviewees of The Momentum Journey. Since I could no longer interview them in person, they have agreed to answer some questions I emailed to them. Each submission in this book contains the original content and has in no way been altered.

The following email was sent to the original sixty-five interviewees:

In advance, thank you for your willingness to help impact the lives of struggling college students and adults in career transition. As you are aware, an unfortunate turn of events occurred when The Momentum Journey RV broke down on September 4th (day one of our journey), thus stopping our physical momentum. We quickly learned that the RV needed a new engine, one that we could not afford to replace. Therefore, we were unable to proceed and had to cancel our scheduled interviews for The Momentum Journey educational documentary. Hopefully, this did not cause any inconvenience for you.

This hiccup, roadblock, obstacle, or whatever you want to term it will not deter me from persevering to fulfill the mission of The Momentum Journey. It is through embracing these challenges in life that build character and make the end result that much more rewarding. Since I am unable to physically interview you for the documentary at this time, I

would like to request that we proceed with your inspirational career story in the below text format. If you are willing to answer the below questions, then I will post your content on our web site (http://www.themomentumjourney.org/).
Feel free to answer any of the following and feel free to add any questions of your own. Here we go!

Name:
Company:
Title:
Industry:
Email:

Please describe your career path in a few paragraphs.

Who were your mentors along the way?
How did they help? Advice they gave?

Please describe your biggest obstacle or fear along the way? How did you overcome the situation?

Please describe your own success habits.

Advice for college students? adults in transition?

People talk about being passionate in life, so how do you define your passion for your career?

Please describe a "Day in The Life of YOU!"

Please list any influential books or other literature you would recommend.

I understand that you have busy schedules, so thank you again for your time. Once enough funds are raised and The Momentum Journey RV (new and improved) is back on the road, I would like to reschedule our original interview for the documentary.

Gratefully,
Rob Lohman – Founder and Chief Motivator

Enjoy the rest of the book.
Thank you again for supporting
The Momentum Journey.

Gratefully,

Rob

Story One

Melanie Gideon
- Original Journeyer

Favorite Quote: "We are the music makers and we are the dreamers of dreams."~Willy Wonka
Favorite Songs: Walk Away, Ben Harper & Change, Blind Melon
Favorite Color: I hate separating the rainbow. ROYGBIV together makes me the happiest.
College: Indiana University, Bloomington Indiana University
Major(s):   Bachelor of Arts in Biology
Minor(s):   Psychology and Public Health
Inspirations: Creative Innovations
Most Impactful Event 2004: The day I realized I had truly regretted something in my life.

My journey has been momentous, but my aspirations have indicated that the only way to go in life is to create my own path. My name is Melanie Gideon and I am a recent graduate from the University of Indiana who technically graduated with biology major, a psychology and public health minor and an unforgettable specialization in preconfusion (a term I have come to define my career prospects and undergraduate motivations with).

Growing up in the suburbs of Detroit Michigan I had all the intentions of going into some kind of medicine, working with kids, putting an end to blindness, and somehow thinking I could also learn to fly, save the world, and cure cancer. Obviously, I came to realize that although these things seemed idealistic, my true happiness may be found in something related but much deeper.

I have a passion for people. I had become the "girl that knows everyone" at IU, and have found a unique sense of energy in my ability to reach new people I meet every day, as well as those I have known my whole life. These people are not my friends because I can take a timed, computer adaptive test, or do the butterfly stroke in my money pit. They are my friends because of the energy I have to motivate them in their own contributions to their own projects. They are inspired by my worldly view and open-minded, hands on experience that enables them to see how their own efforts are of value.

I will not settle for the beaten path of my peers. I refuse to receive my degree in biology and then get lost in the world, working for someone else whose dream I am fulfilling. I will not allow my intensely creative motivation to be swept aside for the sake of starting out. I will not accept a job simply to get by. I will create my path continuing to inspire those who have settled. Those who have become content in finding their small niche, while I foster the intent of creating a new niche.

Without hesitation, I can say that I have a talent. I make people feel important because I care about their motivation. I will not judge a new acquaintance at face value, or believe that what I see is what I get, because I am an exceptional, insightful, mind who has endured more in my life than others much older.

I am fortunate to say that I have traveled to distant third world countries several times, and held the hands of dying children with HIV who have no conception of our world of electronics and Nintendo systems. I have frolicked through the villages of the French Riviera, and sipped wine with near royalty. I have overcome handicapping surgeries, and witnessed the deaths of many loved ones. I have spent weeks inside the depths of the Grand Canyon, hung out with famous musicians, touched the equator, and slept alone, under the stars in the center of a busy capital city in central America. I have started new student organizations and won awards for being a class clown, but never have I answered to a title that even came close to describing who I was as a person.

I have been given a sort of a beaten path, but decided I'd rather not take it. I'm creating my own path and know that it will only be as amazing as the energy and imagination behind it.

Story Two

Aric Geesaman
- Original Journeyer

Favorite Quote: "We make a living by what we get, we make a life by what we give. "   - Sir Winston Churchill

Favorite Songs: Flaming Lips, "Do you Realize?" Gary Jules, "Mad World" U2, "Bad" and when Michael Bolton sings When a Man Loves a Woman...for me it just doesn't get any better than that! (Quote from Office Space, if you were worried I was being serious)

Favorite Color: All the colors of the ocean

College: Indiana University, Bloomington Indiana University

Major(s):   Bachelor of Arts in Biology

Minor(s):   Psychology

Inspirations: First and foremost, my family and all those I love, and after that, it
can honestly be anything that hits me just right

Most Impactful Event 2004:   Finding true disappointment within myself, and finding I couldn't help some of the people closest to me...some things just can't be fixed, and some wounds will never heal

I am one of those people you call a "people person." I love people. I always have. I love doing things for people, especially things that make them feel good, or more importantly, things that make them feel better about themselves.

I grew up in a divided family, not only through divorce, but also through geographic distance.

For a great deal of my young adult life my parents lived in different states. This was not an easy thing to deal with, especially once I started getting active in sports and other school ventures in junior high and high school. As difficult as it was, I always knew my families loved me, and I had a very fortunate life. Right when I moved to college, my families moved even further away, leaving me a 7 hour drive to get home, which ever way I chose to go. This was ok, though, because I was doing what I loved doing...meeting people.

My freshman year I met more people than just about everyone on my floor knew combined. They were always astonished about how many people I knew. Though my best friends were those I met freshman year, for the most part, I continued to meet as many people as I possibly could throughout my college career. Just meeting people wasn't enough, though; I had to be doing something for someone. Then I did something I always wanted to do...I started taking martial arts.

It seems a far cry from helping people at first, learning martial arts, but I saw it for what I would allow me to do in the long run...teach others the knowledge I had gained. I wasn't going to teach them how to fight, because that's not really what I learned in the martial arts. I was going to teach them to believe in themselves, to have confidence in their ability to do what they had to do in any situation, whether their life or a grade depended on it. I was teaching them about responsibility, and self-reliance. I was teaching young women how to potentially fight off a rapist, and at the same time, teaching them how to feel better about who they were as people, and how to follow paths in life that would give them the most meaning. I was helping people feel good about themselves. From then on, I was hooked. I knew I wanted to help people.

Like a hand full of my classmates, I just recently graduated with a great degree from a major university (Biology, from Indiana University, with a minor in Psychology) and found that I had no idea what I really wanted to do with it. Actually, I started feeling clueless at the end of my junior year, but thought maybe something would spark my interest during my senior year and I'd figure out what I wanted to do. That didn't exactly happen. What did happen is I made a giant list of things I knew I didn't want to do...to at least get that out of the way. All I knew was that I wanted to help people in creative, fun and engaging ways.

I originally came to school, like so many of my peers, to get the knowledge I needed to become a doctor. I thought I could help cure some terrible disease, or help a family make an informed decision about an ill loved one. I loved the idea of helping people day in and day out, but quickly became disenchanted with it when I found out that I could help people in myriad different ways, and decided being a doctor wasn't really for me (besides that, I wasn't the best at organic chemistry, so my decision came hand-in-hand with the "weeding" out process for those of us who only got "decent" grades in chemistry and the like). I stuck with my major though, because I loved classes like genetics, microbiology and molecular biology.

The problem I was now facing was that I had no real output for all that knowledge I had gained. What in the world was I going to do with what I knew about reverse transcriptase, secondary estrogen receptors and the three-dimensional structure of a ribosome??? Well, sadly, nothing...yet. But along came The Momentum Journey. Melanie Gideon called me up one afternoon to tell me all about a meeting she just had with her instructor, Rob Lohman, and how excited she was about the project he was starting. She told me all about it and asked me if I'd like to go on The Momentum Journey. Of course I said "yes." It was a chance for us to not only get out and see the beautiful country that we live in, but to meet some incredible people along the way, and more importantly, it would give us a chance to meet and help people just like ourselves. I finally was going to get my chance to make a difference in a perfect stranger's life...I was going to help people.

I might not be saving their lives, but I was going to try to point them in the best direction to get started. We were going to get the chance to be creative, and educate others in fun, engaging ways about how to wade through the fog of confusion and indecision that we often find ourselves in not only in college, but also in the so-called "real world" where everything you do supposedly matters even more.

I've been through some very difficult times in my life, and witnessed some things that were not easy to deal with. I've had a lot of fun in my life, and I've also shed a lot of tears, just like every other human on the planet. I'm not great at everything, but I am very good at a few things. I can help people to understand how amazing they really are and I can motivate them to embrace their dreams and work towards them, even when I'm confused about my own. I can share with them my own experiences and whatever wisdom I have attainted in the 22 short years of my life. I can help people, whether they really need it or not. I don't know what kind of career I want, other than to say I want to make sure that, along the way, I make a difference in a few people's lives.

The Momentum Journey isn't just a project; it's a reflection on life. We all need to find a direction for our journey, for our energy, and we have to put all we have into making it happen...and once we do that, the momentum will carry us to places we didn't even see in our dreams.

Story Three

Allen Tappe
- The Tappe Group

"My biggest obstacle in life is my reluctance to tell people no. After seeing it as a threat to my personal health and integrity, I begin to embrace it as an essential to building trust-based relationships."

I discovered Allen Tappe through my mother. She raved about his motivational training sessions he would present to her real estate company, Williams Trew Real Estate in Fort Worth, Texas. Every time my mom listened to Allen she enthusiastically called to share her newfound inspirations with me.

I contacted Allen on February 27th, 2004 to discuss his participation in the documentaries. Without hesitation he agreed. He said "....anything to help motivate young students in their pursuit for passion."

Enjoy the inspirational story of Allen Tappe!

Name: Allen Tappe

Company: The Tappe Group

Title: President

Industry: Professional Speaking, Training,
                      and Coaching

Please describe your career path in a few paragraphs.

From the very beginning, my career path has been in the field of sales. I began as a twelve year old selling "Spud Nuts" door to door. From that humble beginning I became a tennis teaching professional which involved selling my teaching skills to the public I sought to serve. After college, I began selling mortgage lending and real estate services. At one stage in my career, I sold "infection control" products to hospitals. I had the opportunity to build a college tennis program where I had to sell top athletes on the dream we had as a program.

For the past decade, I have been involved in selling professional speaking, training, and coaching services. The common element in all of my career paths and pursuits is the element of selling. My definition of selling is "mastering the art of influencing the thinking of people is such a way as to help them choose". My understanding and acceptance of my fundamental need to master the selling dimension of life has contributed greatly to whatever success I have experienced.

Who were your mentors along the way? How did they help? Advice they gave?

My high school tennis coach played I significant role as mentor in my life. He helped me to understand the significant role integrity plays in life. He also modeled it for me. He also taught me a great deal about team and teamwork. I was also mentored by my father-in-law who taught me the importance of being true to yourself and to your dreams. He led a balanced life and did not have the need to compare himself to anyone. I have been mentored by countless others in my life particular through their authorship. I am a voracious reader and so people like Viktor Frankl, John

Wooden, Stephen Covey, Jeremy Rifkin and Philip Yancey, I count as mentors. The ever Present Mentor I have in my life is the love of Jesus. His Father and His Holy Spirit provide my center: identity, purpose, and security.

Please describe your biggest obstacle or fear along the way? How did you overcome the situation?

My biggest obstacle in life is my reluctance to tell people no. After seeing it as a threat to my personal health and integrity, I begin to embrace it as an essential to building trust-based relationships.

Please describe your own success habits.

I have an overall Life Plan that I purpose each year. I have now for over 25 years. I don't begin with my Business Plan and then ask my life to fit into it. I begin with conviction and vision for my life and then I fit my Business Plan into it.

Advice for college students? adults in transition?

Accept and embrace selling as being your primary and foundational career. You have to master the art of influencing the thinking of others about you. Selling you is your responsibility. No one else will ever be able to sell you like you. Remember, selling is a science based in numbers. Don't get frustrated in having to "sell" a lot of people about you along the way.

People talk about being passionate in life, so how do you define your passion for your career?

My passion is in helping other people clarify, pursue, and realize their intentions. The more I am able to help others realize their dreams the more I realize my own.

Please describe a "Day in The Life of YOU!"

I begin early with Praise. I spend about twenty-five minutes in Yoga inspired stretching and exercise. Often I do some cardio in the morning. I spend time with the Bible, my journal, and other inspirational material when I am on my game. I have breakfast with my wife of 32 years. I try to encourage my grandchildren before I leave to pursue my day. I spend my days in a variety of expressions of coaching others. I usually begin the important work with my family at home by about 6:00pm. I am in bed by 10:00pm on weekdays. I often play tennis on weekends and enjoy the fellowship of my church family on Sundays.

Please list any influential books or other literature you would recommend.

Let me refer you to my website for a booklist that I keep available, www.tappegroup.com.

Story Four

Brad Cunningham
- eBridge Technologies, Inc.

"If you are not passionate about what you do and do not give 100% of yourself to whatever career you have chosen, then Why are you doing it? We spend almost our entire lives working, if you cannot do it to the best of your ability, that means you have spent the majority of your life not doing your best."

I discovered an article about Brad Cunningham in the April 2004 Special Makeover Issue of Entrepreneur Magazine. The article discussed Brad's decision to leave the Marines and National Guard after nine years of service to follow a new passion. After contacting Brad to discuss his participation in our documentaries, he requested an email with more information about The Momentum Journey. A few days later I received the following email from Brad:

"Rob, I would be honored to be a part of this...in as many aspects and parts as possible. It sounds like a great product and is something that I have already been involved in, with the limited times I have had the opportunity to speak with college students in the past. There is definitely something missing in the life of college students today, lack of perspective, too narrow focused, and too much worth put into GPA in comparison to inner-abilities and strengths,,,to name a few. Looking forward to it."

Enjoy the inspirational story of Brad Cunningham!

Name: Braddock G. Cunningham

Company: eBridge Technologies Inc

Title: President

Industry: Computer Software

Please describe your career path in a few paragraphs.

After spending the first years of my career in the military and then the utility industry in managing project initiatives, I recognized the opportunities for growth in information technology (IT). Having a keen interest in process automation and workflow processes, I realized the tremendous benefits that these cutting edge technologies could provide across numerous industries. I took on numerous projects as an independent contractor to explore in depth the possibilities of the process automation tools. During this period, it became obvious that process automation software could provide tremendous benefits to companies. Best of all, these applications could be developed comparably quickly when I applied my project management skills and logical thinking that was developed during my military service and the MBA program.

Bootstrapping your own business without any outside financial investment is challenging. In order to present the correct image to the potential customer, the company had to appear large and established. So with two employees and one client, I began the launch of Cunningham IBS as a leading provider of custom Lotus applications in 1996. To overcome many obstacles, I concentrated much of IBS's image building through my reputation as an expert instructor of IBM and Lotus technologies. Without any advertising budget to speak of, I was able to gain First Union, Ahold and International Paper as clients and expanded to also include Oracle training and consulting services.

Upon the sell of the majority of Cunningham IBS to Diversified Computer Consultants for 3x revenues, eBridge Technologies was born. The new strategy included building a much larger and scalable business. As eBridge, the strategy was to focus only on recurring revenue sources, i.e. packaged software product sales and ongoing licensing programs. I invested heavily into the company to develop its own line of software products based on past successful custom development projects. The risks were huge over the course of 2000 and 2001. In 2000 I invested over $250,000 as seed capital to get eBridge off the ground, which was the majority of the money received for the sale of IBS, so needless to say, things were tight on all fronts. While at the same time, the economy was beginning to show signs of slowing down and the stock market was declining and still, no outside funding.

By the end of 2001, eBridge had indeed morphed itself into a software product company, had actually lowered its need for resources and was increasing revenues. eBridge's software products had proven invaluable to Fortune 500 clients, and the recurring revenue model had been proven successful. By the end of 2002, eBridge would turn a profit of over $100,000 and record revenue growth of over 20% for the third year in a row and be one of less than 10 companies selected by IBM to have a software product listed as one of IBM's solution proven packages. Today, after only six (6) years in operation and without external funding, eBridge has clients throughout the world and supports enterprise applications for companies such as Liz Claiborne, Springs Industries and Fuji Photo Film.

Who were your mentors along the way?   How did they help? Advice they gave?

I did not have many mentors during my early years, but I hope others do have that opportunity. I was on my own from an early age. I knew I had to make it on my own. After leaving the Marine Corps, I put myself through college, which resulted in a pretty heavy amount of debt and working fulltime in the HVAC industry. Pretty funny in some ways, I remember needing to go to the library many times during college, but I was working emergency service for SEARS Service, which gave me the flexibility I needed, but an income amount that I had to have in order to make ends meet. Many nights, I drove to the library in the work van, smelling of fuel oil, and then getting the weird looks from the normal college students in the library when I went in to do my work in between service calls.

So it was difficult for me to ever fit in with other students, I was older than them and had my military background and fulltime job that all served to set me apart from my college peers. Maybe my background is what has led to my extreme sense of self-responsibility. There were a couple professors I had that could be thought of as mentors in some ways, especially my senior seminar professor, Dr. Stanton. It wasn't so much what I learned in the class, as it was how he approached the class. He really did a lot to run the class in a way that made you feel you were truly a part of everything…on the same level.

I would also have to give a lot of credit to the people I worked with during my time in the HVAC industry, my fellow technicians at SEARS. Here I was, 20 years younger than the average age, doing very skilled work, and going to college, etc.. I was treated by almost everyone there with respect and trust, which really helped me a lot in my development and self-reliance. I would also have to give the same type of credit to many senior NCOs and officers I served with in the Marine Corps, almost everything that I hold high in my life was either learned or reinforced by these fellow Marines.

Please describe your biggest obstacle or fear along the way? How did you overcome the situation?

Not being taken seriously, especially upon entering the world of an entrepreneur. Almost bar none, people questioned my abilities, due to my age and background. I did not fit the "profile" of what other business leaders felt was required to be successful. Word of advice to others – don't believe that kind of thinking! Wish I could provide some magic word, but the reality was that only very hard work and sacrifice has allowed me to overcome many obstacles. It is easy to become jealous or resentful of others, who seem to have more given to them or at least achieve more easily…but you can still do it! As part of an answer for the question below, my advice would be to believe in yourself! I say this especially because as you become successful other people will let you down.

One of the hardest things I have had to deal with over the last 10 years is how people around me that I trusted changed. No one else will understand what you have gone through to become successful, people become jealous, everyone thinks they can do it better or they want it for themselves. A great quote I have had to keep close to my heart over the years is that "The holy passion of friendship is so sweet and so steady and loyal and enduring a nature that it will last through a whole lifetime, if not asked to lend money." By Mark Twain. It is so true, when you are starting out it is easy to have friends and work together to make something happen, but once you make the commitment and sacrifice to move ahead, you will be surprised how many "friends" will no longer be there. When you ask friends to invest not just money, but time and effort on your behalf, you will see what true friends really are.

Please describe your own success habits.

Perseverance
Belief in myself and my abilities...and a CLEAR knowledge of right and wrong
Always trying to do something the best!

People talk about being passionate in life, so how do you define your passion for your career?

If you are not passionate about what you do and do not give 100% of yourself to whatever career you have chosen, then **Why** are you doing it? We spend almost our entire lives working, if you cannot do it to the best of your ability, that means you have spent the majority of your life not doing your best. I know a lot of people like to talk about how work is "not" their life, that home and family is what is really important. While there is no denying that your family should be the most important thing in your life, what you do as a career is incredibly important and to slight it, is to slight yourself.

I have seen so many people go through their work life half-speed, and justifying it by their belief in 'work' not being what is really important…but if you live your life that way, what else in your life do you less than your best? How do you tell the difference, once you begin living that way?

To me, work is life, it is what we do, I do not make a distinction between my "work" life and my "home" life, it is all my life and I try and do everything in my life the best I can! If you do that, everything else will take care of itself and no matter what you will know you gave it your all.

Please describe a "Day in The Life of YOU!"

Hmm..tough one.   Maybe I should give you an example of some days I have had and that anyone going down the same road as I have may encounter.

8am:

Arrive at the office by 8am

Do admin tasks for a couple hours (checks, bills, invoices, etc…)

10am:

Put together a couple new press releases, have a conference call with a business partner

11am:

Speak with a couple customers, help to resolve some support issues…

1pm:

Grab quick lunch..late..

2pm:

Work with an employee on some issues

Continue working on a support issue, follow up on sales prospects

4pm:

Put together sales contract for a project that I have been trying to sell for many months

Go back and forth with the client on pricing and contract wording

5pm:

Call the law firm to get the contract reviewed

5:30pm:

Do a statement of overdue invoices, get with our operations manager to see about resolving the past due accounts

6:30pm:

Respond to a survey and emails

7:30pm:

Eat dinner, smoke a cigar…call a potential investor to discuss the company in hopes of them investing into the company

9pm:

Get a page on my cell phone with an urgent support problem

10pm:

Meet a representative from our computer center at the data center at 10pm to resolve the problem

12pm:

Work on a response to the customer and then sit down to brainstorm some new development work

2am:

Go to sleep! Sleep fast.

Please list any influential books or other literature you would recommend.

Angels & Demons
The DaVinci Code
The Marine Corps Way
PICK A BETTER COUNTRY: An Unassuming Colored
Guy Speaks His Mind About America

Story Five

Greg King
- The BIG Balloon
Communications, Inc.

"I love being successful. I love living life to the fullest. I hate creating limitations based on fear, so I banish fear from my life. I hate boundaries. Those that prevent me from being and becoming the man that God wants me to be from moment to moment. We must set goals that lead to greatness. I don't mean monetarily. I mean fullness. Life's too short to be short sighted. Get up!"

I discovered Greg King in an article titled "The Power of Property" in the March 2004 Issue of Black Enterprise Magazine. Greg discussed his passion for real estate and marketing.

After emailing Greg an invitation to participate in our documentaries, he responded with the following email on April 21st, 2004:

"Rob, This sounds quite interesting. Do you have a website that I can view? I definitely believe in encouraging college students and support lofty organizations..."

Enjoy the inspirational story of Greg King!

Name: Greg King

Company: The BIG Balloon Communications, Inc.

Title: Ring Leader

Industry: Communications, Marketing

Please describe your career path in a few paragraphs.

Our goal as a company is create compelling marketing programs to reach a broad cross sector of consumers. We don't believe in designing cookie cutter programs that may appear to be winners in reaching targeted consumers, we consistently challenge ourselves to be better and create platforms that connect with consumers in an authentic way. Lately, our focus has been to develop new technology tools to connect with young (12 – 38) consumers.

Many larger consumer product and entertainment companies seek out established marketing firms to drive their marketing efforts targeting niche consumers (the young, ethnic and urban demo); however, what they fail to realize is that firms like mine with a creative, diverse and highly educated team each born in an urban setting understands the drivers that push these consumers to purchase, respond or act on a given message.   The deciding factor for who gets the accounts shouldn't be a question of BIG verses small.

Who were your mentors along the way? How did they help? Advice they gave?

I am African American.   My team is very diverse featuring Asian, Hispanic and African American people. We work well together. Most of my education came from being in diverse environments and learning from a natural and spiritual place.   It came from observing, excepting, readjusting and being committed to gaining understanding minus judgment.

In the literal sense of mentors, I had my parents. Two people who pushed me and my brothers to strive for excellence. In business, I had people like Vince Manze at NBC and Leslie Perlman at FOX make a commitment to get me on their teams which lead to my success at the studio level.

Please describe your biggest obstacle or fear along the way? How did you overcome the situation?

Being an entrepreneur is challenging. Daily you spend 100 percent of your day worrying or you can make the conscious decision to think positive and flush fear down the toilet. Each day I make choice to be successful. Each day I focus on success.

Please describe your own success habits.

See above.

Advice for college students? Adults in transition?

Get up every day! I know what this means to you. I'll leave it up to you to define what this means to you in your life.

People talk about being passionate in life, so how do you define your passion for your career?

I love being successful. I love living life to the fullest. I hate creating limitations based on fear, so I banish fear from my life. I hate boundaries. Those that prevent me from being and becoming the man that God wants me to be from moment to moment. We must set goals that lead to greatness. I don't mean monetarily. I mean fullness. Life's too short to be short sighted. Get up!

Please describe a "Day in The Life of YOU!"

A lot of moves. Right now, life is a hustle. Tomorrow, it won't be.

Story Six

Jennifer Roitman
- Head Games

"I live for that"A-Ha!" moment. The athlete who tells me

they have just done a skill that they have been afraid of for so long, that's my passion. The athlete who finally understands the difference between nerves and excitement and uses that excitement as fuel to help them do very well in a competition, that's my passion."

I discovered Jennifer Roitman in the March 2004 Issue of Entrepreneur Magazine. Jennifer had interned with Head Games at the Phoenix location. Because of her inspirational internship, Roitman wanted to expand the business into Boston and convinced the owners with determination to open a Boston office. Wow!

When I spoke with Jennifer about the guiding principles behind our documentaries she exploded with excitement. This young lady was full of so much joy for living life that it was contagious.

Enjoy the inspirational story of Jennifer Roitman!

Name: Jennifer Roitman

Company: Head Games

Title: Mental Toughness Trainer

Industry: Sport Psychology

Please describe your career path in a few paragraphs:

Growing up, gymnastics was my life. It was who I was. If I wasn't in school, I was at the gym. I had always wanted to have the chance to compete on a college gymnastics team and was fortunate enough to be able to have had that chance at the University of Vermont. During my sophomore year, I slipped off of the beam while practicing for our upcoming ECAC championship on a skill that had been the most consistent part of my routine for the last 5 years. In that one slip, I ended up blowing out my knee almost completely and had to have major reconstructive surgery to repair the damages. I was beyond crushed. After being evaluated, my orthopedist, with whom I had been with since the age of 12, asked me if I was going to finally end my gymnastics career. He couldn't believe it when I told him that I had no intentions of quitting. He then told me that if I did not want to stop doing gymnastics, he would have to send me to a knee specialist. I was lucky to have been referred to a wonderful doctor who performed the surgery.

My rehabilitation was very intense and difficult. There were plenty of times that I wondered if my gymnastics was worth the pain I was in both physically and mentally from this injury…and every time I did, deep down my heart told me that I wasn't ready to be done with the sport yet. I had plenty of people around me who told me it was okay if I wanted to "retire" and that with an injury like mine, it wouldn't be surprising if I were to do so. It's funny in retrospect. I can remember thinking to myself that if I knew I could make it back, the people around me should back my decision. In truth, aside from my parents and my physical therapist, I was alone. Even with all of the negativity around me, I ended up making it back for my senior year and ended my career the way I wanted to.

I am a firm believer that you can learn from all of life's experiences, including the one's that you may perceive as being a bad experience. Even in the darkness there is light!   At that time, I was a Psychology major without a focus. My injury and my eventual comeback led me down the path to Sport Psychology. I decided during my junior year that I wanted to work with athletes who were coping and coming back from injuries and be that strength or catalyst that athlete's need to help them push through their obstacles to make it back to where they want to be. I could have used that! I applied and was accepted into graduate school and began my career in the field of Sport Psychology. While in school, I did my practicum at a local private sport psychology practice in Phoenix called Head Games. The relationship I had with the Head Games staff was so good that when I moved back to the east coast after graduation, I helped to open up the east coast office of Head Games and am currently working as a Mental Toughness Trainer for athletes, coaches and parents nationwide.

Who were your mentors along the way? How did they help? Advice they gave?

I have had a few people along the way that have helped to shape my career path in one way or another. First and foremost are my parents. I'll be the first to admit that Sport Psychology is not your typical career path. When I tell people that I am a Mental Toughness Trainer and work with athletes on the mental side of sports, I get a lot of blank stares. When I told my parents that this was what I wanted to do, they were so excited and thought it was a great idea. They have been so supportive of me as I try to create business and expand with Head Games. They have supported me from the day one and continue to help support me as I pursue this field of work. They could see my dream along with me and have been willing to do what it takes to help me get there. Words can't even describe how much that means to me.

I would not be where I am today without Alison Arnold and Chris Dorris, who co-founded Head Games. When I found out that I was going to be doing my practicum with them while in grad school, I had no idea that it would take me as far as it has. They took me in and guided me as I figured out how I wanted to be involved in this field. More than that, they have each in their own ways have taught me about confidence and how what I do truly makes a difference in people's lives. They have always supported me and encouraged me to go out there be myself.

Please describe your biggest obstacle or fear along the way. How did you overcome this situation?

I am in a field that does not have many already established jobs. It is still up and coming and will take some more time to become more mainstream. As such, the best way to get into the field is to create your own position. So, the biggest obstacle for me so far has been to create my own niche and to build a job myself. In this job, I don't work in your typical office setting with lots of co-workers around you. Sometimes it is difficult to keep up my motivation. The biggest fear I have had is questioning my competence in certain situations.

When this happens, I take a step back and remember that I have the training, hands-on experience and the know how to make this a success. I have learned to take some of my own "medicine." When I work with an athlete who is dealing with fears, one of the skills I teach is the power of positive self-talk. No one can think more than one thought at one time. When you think negative, you have no room to allow the positive thoughts to come through. By beating down these negative thoughts, I make room for the positive ones. I found that the best way for me to conquer this obstacle and fear has been to jump right in, kick those negative thoughts to the curb, make a plan of action and then begin to take the steps to complete the task at hand. I know that I have a valuable service to provide. I think about of all of the people who I have been able to help in the past and use that to fuel my future!

Please describe your own success habits.

In a situation like mine where you have 2 jobs, you have to have great time management skills. My work with Head Games is about 4 hours during weeknights and weekends when necessary. Not a whole lot of time when you think about it. It's important to stay focused during the time that you have with whatever career you choose as time has a funny way of slipping by.
Also, and probably most important, is remembering that I have a very valuable service to provide to others. When you are clear with your services and find a way to present them effectively, the business comes much easier.

Advice for college students? Adults in transition?

Choosing a career is sometimes not an easy thing. I wasn't one of those people that knew that they wanted to be a doctor or a lawyer. Until my junior year I did not know what I wanted to be doing. I have been very lucky to find a career that I enjoy. In addition to my work with Head Games, I also work as a Career Counselor. I meet with people all the time who are in the midst of a career change. Our society is so focused on work and career that when someone is unsure as to what they want to do, they may feel, in some way, that there is something wrong with them. That could not be further from the truth.   My advice to college students is to take full advantage of their college or university's career services office.

When I was in school, I did not even know that something like that existed until it was too late. They are full of excellent advisors, helpful career directing workshops and maybe even campus recruitments to help you land that first job after college.

For adults in transition, there are a few things that I would recommend. First, if they attended college, they can still take advantage of their school's career services office. Most of them do cater to alumni! Additionally, if their state has an established One-Stop career center system, I would very much recommend that they look into services to help them with their career transition.

For both groups, the key is to network. 80% of all jobs come from networking, yet it can be the most underutilized technique when it comes to career advice and job seeking. A grad school professor of mine once told me that it is whom you know to get you there and what you know to keep you there. How true that is!

People talk about being passionate in life, so how do you define you passion for your career?

Everyone has a different idea of what passion is. My passion for my career comes from direct experience. After my knee injury and the hard times that I endured when in the midst of my comeback, I learned to look inside myself to find the motivation and desire to push me through each and every day. I want to serve as a catalyst for change for others in a variety of situations. Now, it's my athletes that continue to provide the fuel for my passion. I live for that "A-Ha!" moment. The athlete who tells me they have just done a skill that they have been afraid of for so long, that's my passion. The athlete who finally understands the difference between nerves and excitement and uses that excitement as fuel to help them do very well in a competition, that's my passion. The student-athlete who realizes that their sport has given them a plethora of transferable skills that can be used in a "real world" environment, that's my passion. Can you tell I love what I do?!

Please describe a "Day in the Life of YOU!"

My job as a Mental Toughness Trainer is not a full time job at the moment. I work during the day as a Career Counselor in the Boston area, a job that I really enjoy. It is my hope to one day be able to combine the two. When I get home in the evenings and on the weekends, that is the time that I meet with my athletes, teams, coaches and parents. It is definitely tough as it creates quite a packed schedule, but it is all worthwhile at the end of the day!

Please list any influential books or other literature you would recommend.

I am the type of person who can find inspiration in even the smallest things. It doesn't take much to inspire me. I've been inspired by books, quotes, songs, stories and even a commercial or two! Any story where I am reading or hearing about a person's ability to comeback to their sport or comeback in life inspires me. It reminds me of my own struggles to make it back in gymnastics while I was in college. When I was having a difficult time with my knee rehabilitation, I found inspiration in the story of skier, Picabo Street. Her story was all over the news as she was planning a comeback from her major knee injury to compete in the 1998 Nagano Olympics. I felt her pain and was captivated by her determination to prove everyone wrong and to go out there and show everyone, including herself, that she belonged there. In one of her interviews, she said, "A tiger hunts best when he's hungry. I'm hungry!" Hence, the tiger she had painted on her helmet. She sure was. I remember being so inspired when she won the Super G! I read her autobiography a few years after that and loved it. So, I would recommend Picabo: Nothing to Hide for anyone looking to be inspired.

Story Seven

Mark Laurie
- Passion Inc.

"Whether you start your own business or work within a big company focus on making change happen and good things should happen. Everybody loves a change agent."

I discovered Mark Laurie's name because he is the Publisher the JobPostings Magazine which is displayed in most college career centers around the country. I used their magazine quite often with students while I was a Career Counselor at Indiana University. Their articles really capture the essence of passion and career direction.

Mark agreed to follow The Momentum Journey in a series of articles once we completed a series of interviews. He was excited about our mission.

Enjoy the inspirational story of Mark Laurie!

Name: Mark Laurie

Company: Passion Inc.

Title: Co-Founder

Industry: Publishing & Software

Please describe your career path in a few paragraphs.

We started Passion Inc. while in university as a way to help finance our education. Since graduating in 1997 we have been working full time to grow the business and now have monthly magazines, websites, and on-line software.

Who were your mentors along the way? How did they help? Advice they gave?

Our mentors have been successful business leaders as well as our parents. Our dad is an entrepreneur so we have grown up in a culture of business. We have never really had formal advice but receive feedback informally that finds its way into our business strategy.

Please describe your biggest obstacle or fear along the way? How did you overcome the situation?

Our biggest fear is that we could go bankrupt one day and lose everything. For that reason we have tried to grow responsibly and keep a close eye on our expenses as well as our revenue growth. Most companies go bankrupt having record sales so watching the bottom line is our main priority.

Please describe your own success habits.

Any success we have is a result of hard work and building a team around ourselves that can help execute our vision.

Advice for college students? adults in transition?

Whether you start your own business or work within a big company focus on making change happen and good things should happen. Everybody loves a change agent.

People talk about being passionate in life, so how do you define your passion for your career?

My passion comes from the satisfaction of taking ideas and transforming them into realities. I love the challenge of making change happen.

Please describe a "Day in The Life of YOU!"

Every day is different but most start around 7:30am and end by 8pm. Much of my time is dealt talking with our people and working on special projects that involve new ideas or new technology. We just rolled out IP phones. It took 3 months of hard work, planning, testing, and trouble-shooting. The same process is also occurring with our websites which are currently being rebuilt and take a lot of time and effort to get right.

Please list any influential books or other literature you would recommend.

Good To Great
SPIN Selling
Max Strategy

Story Eight

Mike Wohl
- bodywisdom media, Inc.

"Once you do it, however, you can't believe it is so easy. It's like jumping into a pool and worrying about how cold it feels on your feet before you go in. Once you're in it, the pool is fine. It's only when you just put a toe in and you fear what the pool will feel like if you jump in that is so hard."

I discovered Michael Wohl in the April 2004 Special Makeover Issue of Entrepreneur Magazine. In the article "For Sanity's Sake" Michael stated that "All work and no play makes a dull entrepreneur, so find a healthy balance between your life and your business."

Michael is passionate about yoga and meditation. His passion is evident in his voice, his spirituality, and his desire to improve the lives of those around him.

Enjoy the inspirational story of Michael Wohl!

Name: Michael Wohl

Company: bodywisdom media, Inc

Title: President

Industry: Video production/distribution

Please describe your career path in a few paragraphs.

I never had a career path per se. In high school and college I was very good at science and math, so I was pushed along the engineering path. I did not realize at all at the time how many opportunities of interest were open. I pursued what I could do well and where I knew I could succeed rather than what I loved. I have an undergraduate degree in Optical engineering (laser physics) and a Masters in Biomedical engineering. As an undergraduate II had received a fifth year scholarship to study classical guitar in Austria for a year as well as history, German, politics and economics (fantastic program at the University of Rochester). As an engineer I had a very limited curriculum and this year opened my eyes to so many ideas and pursuits that I fell in love with. Although I 'came alive' intellectually I still pursued the practical course of getting a PhD in Biomendical Engineering. I stopped after my masters because I realized that at the age of 23 it was better to take a risk studying something I loved and fall on my face when young rather than when I was older and had a family.

I decided to get a PhD in international relations and was accepted to one of the best schools for this, the Fletcher School of Law and Diplomacy. I did not receive financial aid, however, and deferred enrollment. I tried to figure out what would make me more 'attractive' for a scholarship and decided to study international relations in Jerusalem, learn Hebrew and Arabic, work on negotiations between Israelis and Palestinians and get some graduate courses under my belt in the subject. After this year, I still did not get any financial aid.

Back in the states, I realized that if I became an engineer I'd never leave because of a nice salary (golden handcuffs). So I tried being a waiter (it was the recession of the early 90's) and failed terribly. Broke and desperate I tried to come up with money for grad school, borrowed money from my brother and began selling candles on college campuses and made great money. I then began making them myself with a friend from college. Within a few years we had over 40 employees, yet I was no closer to being a professor in international relations as I wanted. Candle making had no passion for me, but was a very successful business. I sincerely believed that business without a passion coming from a deeper place was far from ideal.

By the late 90's, I dedicated myself to pursuing a lifelong passion of practicing internal, somatic arts - mainly tai chi and yoga (a ruptured disc helped focus my attention on taking care of myself). I sold the candle company to just focus on my practice (We spent very little money, rented a small place and were very frugal). I was unsure how I would make a living.

Two years later, as an engineer and yoga practitioner I saw an opportunity for developing fitness DVDs in a new and innovative way that would give tremendous value and flexibility to the user. I formed my present company 4 years ago and have become one of the largest independent producers/distributors of fitness DVDs in the country. It has come solely out of my passion for helping people heal themselves through yoga, as yoga has transformed my life.

Who were your mentors along the way? How did they help? Advice they gave?

Dealing mostly in theoretical physics, I had very few mentors along the way in business. All the people that had MBAs said on numerous occasions that if 'I knew what I was doing', such as if I had an MBA, I never would have succeeded since so much of what I did was unorthodox. My present business included. My business partner for my first business was and is a dear friend with whom I could discuss and argue about anything and everything. This process of open, relatively egoless argumentation and discussion was my mentor. I always wished I had an older mentor who I could trust thoroughly with whom I could consult. In practice, however, I ignored most everyone's advice (sometimes to my detriment, more often to my benefit) and let the merits of any situation unfold themselves to me through discussion.

Please describe your biggest obstacle or fear along the way? How did you overcome the situation?

Getting started in business was the hardest. I was desperate, otherwise I don't know if I would have had the courage to do so. Once you do it, however, you can't believe it is so easy. It's like jumping into a pool and worrying about how cold it feels on your feet before you go in. Once you're in it, the pool is fine. It's only when you just put a toe in and you fear what the pool will feel like if you jump in that is so hard. I am always amazed at people who can just walk up to a pool or lake and jump in without checking the water. I can't.

Once I was in business, my fear was always that I was going out of business next month. To this day, with two very successful businesses behind me, I have not gotten rid of that fear. In many ways it has benefited me (fear is not necessarily a bad thing - it prevents us from petting tigers, for instance - keeps us alert). Since I think I have this fear that the sky is falling down, I plan for numerous contingencies, always searching for holes in the business and suring them up. Fear also makes me try 5 different initiatives with the hope that one will succeed and save my business that might fail next month. More often than not more than one initiative works and the business grows and has never failed. The one bit of advice my dad gave me in life that has really helped here is "Plan for the worst, but hope for the best".

Fear to me is not necessarily something to be overcome, as much as managed and understood. Knowing your weakness, I believe, can become one's greatest strength.

Please describe your own success habits.

1) Always save much more than you spend. 2) Discover your real, true passion and pursue it. 3) Prioritize family first if you want a family. Everything else in life comes and goes, 4) Know your strengths and weaknesses - acknowledge the former and respect the latter. and 5) Adjust your life accordingly.

Advice for college students? adults in transition?

For myself, taking a wide range of subjects and pursuing what I loved was key. If anything feels like 'work' ie. you really don't care about the outcome, get off that path and search out another if you don't have kids, a mortgage, etc. DO NOT TAKE ON ANY DEBT WHATSOEVER, except a mortgage and student loans if necessary.

For all people I would say, time goes by so quickly, including the difficult times. Just point yourself in a direction you love, work through it the best you can and always look for the light at the end of the tunnel - sometimes it's not so obvious and it might not be the light you were expecting.

People talk about being passionate in life, so how do you define your passion for your career?

I love yoga. It has transformed my life. This is a central passion. Helping others heal themselves is a passion (I have not experienced anything that makes me feel more whole and connected to others). This business of being able to affect so many people in such a positive way feels like the culmination of my search.

Please describe a "Day in The Life of YOU!"

I have tried to plan my life so that at this point I can see my children grow (right now I have a 17-month old girl). I usually wake up and 7am and play with her until 9am. I work at home usually until 3pm (with my daughter desperately trying to rewrite and send emails on my lap half the time - dangerous work hazard!) at 3pm I do a couple hours of yoga - if baby nap schedules permit (I have a small house) - and then I work another hour or two until dinner. I can't stand the idea of getting an office outside the house where I couldn't play with my daughter from time to time during the day. This is the point around which I orient my life.
In the evenings I'll either do more yoga and/or play classical guitar.

During productions, life is crazy - non-stop morning to night work for weeks and months.

Please list any influential books or other literature you would recommend.

The Art of Happiness - Dalai Lama
Thoughts Without a Thinker - Mark Epstein
Destructive Emotions - Dalai Lama
Worldly Philosophers - Heilbrunner
The Tree of Yoga - BKS Iyengar
The Yoga Sutras (1st and 2nd chapters) - Patanjali

Story Nine

Paulo Filgueiras
- Paulo Filgueiras Photography

"No matter what you do, when you do with your heart and a smile in your soul you are already a winner. I do photography for these reasons. I love it. It touches my soul. So I think, I can touch people's souls throughout my photography."

I discovered Paulo Filgueiras in the March / April 2004 Issue of Digital Photo Pro Magazine. The article "Fresh Fashions" stated that Paulo is making a mark in the New York fashion scene through inventiveness and a driving desire to create a new look in his images. Paulo stated "Photography is my life. It's all I ever wanted to do. It's a passion."

We had many enjoyable conversations while trying to schedule a convenient date for the interview. Paulo was busy traveling around the world to exotic locations for his photography shoots, but we finally nailed down an interview date of November 11th.

Enjoy the inspirational story of Paulo Filgueiras!

Name: Paulo Filgueiras

Company: Paulo Filgueiras Photography

Title: Photographer

Industry: Fashion

Please describe your career path in a few paragraphs.

It was a long road to the point I am now, marked by many events that at time made me even think of giving up. But, here I am writing these lines telling a story. I started my photography in my home country Brazil. Born in Rio de Janeiro, I grew up by the shore. When I took my first class for photography, at ABAF (Brazilian Association for Photography Art), I was very young and had not much budget to invest. So I decided to use the natural resources available to practice my photography, and found in the Surf industry a niche to show my work and build up from there. So I did. Got better, and consequently the industry star to ask me to shoot some surf wear.

From that moment on I did never stop to target my work to the Fashion industry. I open a great studio space near the shore so I could shoot fashion and keep surf scene to my reach. For a good while I was shooting for magazines of both industries and expending my advertising clients. It was all good until we had a major turn-around in Brazil's economy and the industry came to a halt. I thought it could be a right moment to come to New York (photo industry main stream). I took classes at SVA extending my technique in studio lighting and fashion. I decided to look for assistant job where I could learn more about the business, acquire better techniques and sustain my living. Time did past by to the moment I was able to have my book together and get my first assignments in NYC.

Who were your mentors along the way? How did they help? Advice they gave?

I never did have a mentor per say. But, I sure did find good people, with good hearts. From photographers I've worked with to people I've met along the way. The best advice was to never give up.

Please describe your biggest obstacle or fear along the way? How did you overcome the situation?

At the beginning I had the language to learn and money was short. It held me back for a good while. You know. I had to start from scratch my career in photography again. I knew it was a matter of time and I just decided to cope with that.

Please describe your own success habits.

Take life one day at a time. Avoid the unnecessary stress and focus on where you want to go and go for it!

Advice for college students? adults in transition?

I've learned in the US that what counts is the voyage not the destination. If so, live for your dreams and make them a worthy experience.

People talk about being passionate in life, so how do you define your passion for your career?

No matter what you do, when you do with your heart and a smile in your soul you are already a winner. I do photography for these reasons. I love it. It touches my soul. So I think, I can touch people's souls throughout my photography.

Please describe a "Day in The Life of YOU!"

My days are quite busy. Sometimes to the extreme. Long days where many tasks are needed to be done, supervised, created and or negotiated. I just try to keep it below the level of stress with good attitude and lots of music. This way I keep my creative side more open for what I really am about, creating unique and striking images.

Please list any influential books or other literature you would recommend.

Let me just name some Artists who I much admire and take inspiration from:
Masters Painters: Dali, Van Gogh, Renoir...
Writers: Gabriel Garcia Marquez, Paulo Coelho, Richard Bach, Saint Exupery...
Visionaries: Da Vinci, Stanley Kubrick, Charlie Chaplin...

Story Ten

Richard Warner
- What's Up Interactive

"Being energetic about it...creative...excited about finding new ways or new thoughts. I think most people who consider themselves to be passionate also realize that this is not something that happens all the time. Passion is when you go home at night and have dreams about something you're working on."

I discovered Richard Warner in the March 2004 Issue of Entrepreneur Magazine. The article discussed Richard's passion to start a business in his home which later outgrew his bedroom, kitchen and den into what you know today as What's Up Interactive.

When I finally contacted Richard about his involvement in our documentaries he replied with "..anything we can do to help."

Enjoy the inspirational story of Richard Warner!

Name: Richard Warner

Company: What's Up Interactive

Title: President

Industry: Interactive ad agency

Please describe your career path in a few paragraphs.

I always wanted to be in broadcasting — at age 6 in northern Ohio, I was collecting TV GUIDE magazines because I was fascinated with the way different stations carried different shows. In college at the University of Georgia, the campus radio station offered to let me read the news once each weekend afternoon, and from there I was hooked.

The weekend work developed into weekday work...which led to a job at the local commercial station. Upon graduation, I landed a plum spot on WSB AM, the dominant AM station in Atlanta and eventually to a competing station across the street.

The local PBS station called me out of the blue and offered up a job hosting a weekly business show, and that led to more part time work at commercial stations in the market.

During all that, I recognized the promise that fax machines (then, a new tool) represented for communication and built a small company that transmitted news releases by fax. We entered Web development in 1995...sold the company in 2000 to a public firm, making me a paper millionaire for a week or two...and bought the company back in 2002.

Along the way, I got married and have two daughters. My family is a treasure.

Who were your mentors along the way? How did they help? Advice they gave?

Oh, yes. There were mentors. A couple in particular, both general managers of the same TV station. The thing was, they enjoyed hearing about my troubles because theirs' were so much worse! In most cases, they had been down a similar road at one time or another and could nod and smile. Now that you ask, it seems like they rarely ponied up advice unless I asked for it. Most of the time, we just talked and it helped. One characteristic that both men share is that they are "real;" no posturing, not a lot of ego. They personify the management style that's currently in style, which I believe the experts are referring to as benevolent leadership.

Please describe your biggest obstacle or fear along the way? How did you overcome the situation?

Oh, man…how much time do you have? Biggest obstacle: growing my own skills so that my business can grow. That encompasses so much territory, from people skills to cash flow to marketing to strategy. I haven't mastered any of it yet. I've gotten better by gradually meeting difficult situations head-on earlier than I used to. Bill Clinton said an effective leader is about 80% nice guy and 20% son of a bitch. That seems to imply that you can't rule with an iron fist, but likewise, you can't avoid the tough decisions. I think we all want to be liked and finding a balance between that and being a pushover is important to anyone's professional life.

Please describe your own success habits.

Well, keeping a list is critical. You can't accomplish things unless you write them down and keep track of them. Otherwise, work will expand to fill the time you have. Also, communicating is a key --- unlike my comments on this page, I try to position my communications here at the company not on "me", but on the readers.

Advice for college students? adults in transition?

I would say be prepared and at peace with the thought that your career will change above and beyond what you see for yourself now. Some people fight that — the concept of reinventing themselves is scary. They're under the mistaken impression that a career is going to go straight up (or, for the pessimist, straight down). Fact is, there will be stages — some successful and some not and you have to be confident that this stage, if it's a bad one, will change. And if it's a good one...well, just know that it will not always be this great...but will once again.

People talk about being passionate in life, so how do you define your passion for your career?

Being energetic about it...creative...excited about finding new ways or new thoughts. I think most people who consider themselves to be passionate also realize that this is not something that happens all the time. Passion is when you go home at night and have dreams about something you're working on.

Please describe a "Day in The Life of YOU!"

Well, every day is different and for the way I'm wired, that's perfect. It might involve shooting a video, or taping a TV show at PBS (where, inevitably, I meet fascinating people)...it could involve designing collateral for my company or working on a new project.

Please list any influential books or other literature you would recommend.

I would say "Five Patterns of Extraordinary Careers," "The Rural Life" by Verlyn Klinkenbourg (NY Times Editorial Board Member), Robert Schuller's autobiography...and for the TV industry enthusiasts, a book called "The Box" by Jeff Kisseloff.

Story Eleven

Seth Resnick
   - Seth Resnick Photography
D-65llc, PixelGenius llc

"Many of us don't start out with much confidence, but we need to project it nonetheless.   Of course I made plenty of mistakes along the way, but I made sure to learn from them and spent a lot of time honing my business skills as well as my photography skills."

I discovered Seth Resnick in the March / April 2004 Issue of Digital Photo Pro Magazine. The article "Great Photographers are Where You Find Them" discussed Seth's career journey as:

"..A student in the 7th and 8th grade, he was confident that he could produce the text of a book about aquariums, but felt he needed to hire a photographer....he learned the going rate for a photographer ran into the several hundreds per day...decided to be his own photographer...Resnick's career as a photographer began right there."

Seth gladly accepted the invitation to participate in our documentaries. He is a very down-to-earth person with a solid foundation a values. This persona is reflected in his photography.

Enjoy the inspirational story of Seth Resnick!

Name: Seth Resnick

Company: D-65llc, PixelGenius llc,
               Seth Resnick Photography

Industry: Photography

Please describe your career path in a few paragraphs.

I started out with an internship at the Syracuse Newspapers after an inspiring semester in London. The internship turned into a job and I stayed there for 5 years honing in on all my skills.

Who were your mentors along the way? How did they help? Advice they gave?

Jay Maisel was and still is my biggest mentor. He taught me the meaning of the word NO and that you were only as good as your last job. Don't sell yourself short and don't do the job unless you are going to do the best that you can.

Please describe your biggest obstacle or fear along the way? How did you overcome the situation?

The fear of going freelance. There was an enormous fear of walking away from a steady paying job at the newspaper. Was I good enough, would I fail or would I flourish?
In the end, your persistence, talent and business skills are the key. You need to believe it is possible to succeed, and then be able to convince others that you can too. Freelancing is not for everyone, but it is not impossible. It requires a particular configuration of skills, and being good at making images is only one small part. In addition you need to have good skills in logistics, marketing, business, and dealing with people, all at the same time.

Marketing is indeed a challenging part of freelancing. Keeping a business going is a never ending effort. Doing a little here and a little there won't cut it. You need to research the clients you want to target and then go after them with a plan. I spend a great deal of time developing clients and making sure I keep them through marketing. Getting and keeping clients can take as much of your time as taking pictures and doing assignments, but it is a part of the equation that you cannot ignore. Work will only come your way if you make it happen. It is my experience that making personal contact is useful if you can do a good job of selling yourself one on one. This is how I've built a business that is both regional, national and international in scope.

Many of us don't start out with much confidence, but we need to project it nonetheless. Of course, I made plenty of mistakes along the way, but I made sure to learn from them and spent a lot of time honing my business skills as well as my photography skills.

Please describe your own success habits.

See above.

Advice for college students? adults in transition?

See above.

People talk about being passionate in life, so how do you define your passion for your career?

There are too many things to do in this world so I wouldn't have chosen photography unless I loved it. I don't ever want to look at my profession as just a job. The passion is the fire that creates creativity and I want to maintain the ability to use my minds eye which only works if I am passionate about my work.

Please describe a "Day in The Life of YOU!"

It is a day just like today. Get up at 4 AM and answer some emails and watch the sunrise. Get my basic work done so that I can focus on creativity for the rest of the day. At days end I have to watch the sun set and I will usually go back to work around 8 PM and work until 11 or so.

Reflections Page

Reflections Page

Appendix I

Phase I: Momentum - An Inspirational Journey (student focused)

The Issue: Traditional and untraditional college students are so focused on triple majoring, double minoring and overcommitting, that they forget about one thing – themselves. It's time to get back to the basics of discovering and pursuing personal dreams. It's time to provide alternative avenues for students to explore their untapped passions. It's time to release their entrepreneurial spirit!

The Mission: The mission of Phase I of The Momentum Journey is to inspire students to be entrepreneurial in discovering their passions and pursuing their dreams in life. This will be accomplished by creating a series of educational documentaries consisting of the following:

- ➤ Interviews with college students discussing their fears associated with career decisions

- ➤ Interviews with college career development centers discussing the services offered to assist students with career decisions

- ➤ Interviews with entrepreneurial minded individuals and everyday people sharing their journeys involved with discovering their career passions

Once the series of educational documentaries is completed, The Momentum Journey will visit colleges and high schools across the country to share experiences from the journey, clips from the inspirational stories of our interviewees, and encourage students to utilize their campus career centers. We will also be hosting tailgate parties during college events.

Phase II: Momentum – The Internship Experience (student focused) - Starts summer after Phase I

Provide a variety of internships for college students in areas of marketing, public relations, web site development/maintenance, video production, and human resources

Phase III: Momentum : Career Services - TBD

Provide career services for the local community at a nominal cost for assistance with resumes, cover letters, personal statements, video mock interviews, job search strategies, salary negotiation strategies, and other career related services.

Phase IV: The Momentum Journey Career Exploration Camp – (nationwide focused) - TBD

Provide a variety of career exploration programs for students and adults facing career transition. Professional career counselors will lead work shops and administer testing materials based on the regulations in place by respective states where the camps will be located.

Appendix II

Dear _____:

I appreciate your willingness to listen to the mission of The Momentum Journey, Inc. – an educational nonprofit organization designed to create career exploration programs, using multimedia productions, for college students and adults in career transition.

As mentioned, I read an inspirational article about you in the _____ issue of _____ Magazine. You mentioned _____ Now that dream is a passionate reality. I believe your story is one that needs to be shared with college students across the country. Please read the following to further understand the mission of Phase I of The Momentum Journey called:

MOMENTUM: AN INSPIRATIONAL JOURNEY

The Issue:

As today's college students prepare for graduation, they seem overwhelmed by their fears associated with choosing the right career path towards success. They are so focused on triple majoring, double minoring and overcomitting, that they forget about one thing – themselves. It's time to get back to the basics of individuality. It's time to explore.

The Mission:

The mission of Momentum is to create a series of educational documentaries designed to inspire students to discover their passions and pursue their dreams in life. This will be accomplished through interviewing college students, career development centers, businesses, and everyday people to understand the "stepping stones" involved in the journey of career paths.
The next phase will involve presenting the documentaries to college students across the country in a motivational forum.

The Goals:

➢ *Establish a nationwide network of people willing to share their experience, strength and hope involved in their journeys of career paths*
➢ *Create inspirational, interactive media outlets for students to visualize the full experience of Momentum*
➢ *Develop college level programs where students can earn credit and explore career interests using the same concepts as Momentum*

The Core Values:

➢ *Dedication to the struggling student and to the financial supporters*
➢ *Rebuild confidence in the possibilities of making dreams become reality*
➢ *Embrace the simple things in life*
➢ *Appreciate the time, effort and input of individuals met on the journey*
➢ *Maintain the momentum and faith necessary to endure the tough times*
➢ *Step beyond your comfort zone. Blaze new trails.*

Hopefully you see the value in your story in relation to the overall mission of Momentum. Are you willing to help keep the momentum going? I would like to discuss this further and schedule an interview for the documentary.

Feel free to contact me via email or via phone at _____. Unless I hear from you prior to _____, I will contact you to follow up. Have a great day.

Gratefully,

Rob Lohman
Founder and Chief Motivator

Appendix III

Sponsorship Levels

In order to attract a variety of sponsors, the below sponsorship levels have been created with unique benefits for each level. (Valued on either financial, service or equipment donations.)

A. $10,001 and beyond

➢ **Prominent logo exposure on the exterior of The Momentum Journey vehicle**

➢ **Interview coverage in the educational documentary and a digital copy of the coverage for your future advertising purposes**

➢ Recognition through nationwide exposure to college students, career development centers, entrepreneurs, and everyday people

➢ Recognition during radio or television interviews

➢ Recognition in published newspaper and magazine articles

➢ Advertising logo on interactive web site with direct link to sponsor's web site

➢ Community recognition as a sponsor of educational career development programs

➢ Name painted inside a 3x3 square inch box on outside of The Momentum Journey vehicle

➢ Acknowledgement as a sponsor on web site

B. $2,001 to $10,000

> **Recognition through nationwide exposure to college students, career development centers, entrepreneurs, and everyday people**

> **Recognition during radio or television interviews**

> **Recognition in published newspaper and magazine articles**

> **Advertising logo on interactive web site with direct link to sponsor's web site**

> Community recognition as a sponsor of educational career development programs

> Name painted inside a 3x3 square inch box on outside of The Momentum Journey vehicle

> Acknowledgement as a sponsor on web site

C. $501 to $2,000

> **Community recognition as a sponsor of educational career development programs**

> Name painted inside a 3x3 square inch box on outside of The Momentum Journey vehicle

> Acknowledgement as a sponsor on web site

D. $100 to $500

> **Name painted inside a 3x3 square inch box on outside of The Momentum Journey vehicle**

> Acknowledgement as a sponsor on web site

E.   Up to $99

> **Acknowledgement as a sponsor on web site**

The above Sponsorship Levels allows for individuals, businesses and organizations to participate in the mission of The Momentum Journey. We want people to believe in and feel comfortable that your hard earned dollars will be put towards enhancing the quality of The Momentum Journey programs.

* The above Sponsorship Program is subject to change, so please visit www.themomentumjourney.org for updates.

Appendix AA

Why would I discuss with you the role alcohol played in my life? It is my belief that by sharing my experience, strength, and hope with you that maybe I could help save you or someone you know the agony I endured for so many years.

This story is mine and mine alone. My story has no reflection upon my family whatsoever. The stories are real. The truth is astonishing.

The Short Version…

I drank. Alcohol ruled my life. I hit my bottom in life. Now I don't drink. Life's incredible. That's it in a nutshell.

The Long Version….

If you are truly interested in how alcohol affected my life, then please continue reading

I grew up with the necessary ingredients to live a great life. My parents displayed unconditional love on a daily basis. They taught me right from wrong. They taught me about God's unconditional love. They were and still are wonderful parents.

There was one thing wrong…I was wired differently than most kids. From the get-go I recall feeling "less than" or "greater than" and nowhere in between. I was the kid with braces, glasses, and a witty sense of humor. I loved being the center of attention to counterbalance my insecurities.

The first time I remember getting drunk occurred during a Christian Youth party. Imagine that! Some kid brought a six-pack of beer and asked me to join him and two cute females in the alley. I drank three. They split the rest. Something magical happened that evening because I changed forever. A light bulb went off. My insecurities vanished for that moment. Self-confidence rose. Alcohol became my subtle master that night.

I know that God's hand rested upon my head during the next fourteen years because I should have died on numerous occasions. And that's no joke.

As we all know, high school can be a tough place to "fit in". Alcohol provided a common bond between social clicks from freshmen to seniors. I found people that drank like me. I also found people that drank worse than me so I would have something to compare my consumption to. Drinking was fun. Drinking was a habit. Drinking was my outlet.

My desire to "fit in" enabled me to become a chameleon in life. I wanted everyone to like me, however I never real felt connected to any social circle. I do not mention this for sympathy but to emphasize the point that the pressures of society can create difficult barriers for individuals to grow and become who they really are. Life should not be about the material concepts, but about the spiritual concepts. Discovering the inner core of self is the most magnificent gift one can give themselves. I did not have this gift until I put the bottle down on June 8, 2001. We'll get into that in a moment.

HIGH SCHOOL YEARS

High school was all about fake id cards, drinking, popularity, and studying enough to get by.   I was placed in all of the accelerated classes which labeled me as one of the "brainiacs".   So I knew I was smart. A friend of mine says "…If you put alcohol and potential in a room together, alcohol will kick potential's ass every time."   This proved to be true during my life until I put the cork in the jug.

When I turned sixteen, my parents went away for the weekend and trusted me to be on good behavior. No more than six hours later, I tried to outrun a policeman through a residential neighborhood exceeding sixty m.p.h. in an attempt to avoid a DUI. Scared beyond belief, I decided to stop the car, throw my hands in the air, and wait for the cuffs. After knocking me around for a few minutes, the officer cited me for speeding, no turn signal, and expired license tags. That's right. I avoided my first DUI. How did I not get a DUI? Who knows except for God.

Throughout junior and senior year in high school, a group of us used to head to a local restaurant during lunch to down two or three long-island iced teas and then head back to school for the remainder of our classes. Drinking was already taking place four or five days/nights a week. It was already a habit. Bad habits are hard to break! Can you relate?

I managed to receive three MIP (minor in possession of alcohol) charges that my parents never found out about. Or maybe they did but never said anything. I guess they know now.

My popularity among various clicks rose to new levels as I joined numerous organizations and clubs in high school. People took to my personality which allowed me to become Senior Class President. I had arrived! Quite a boost to the ego and my bigshotism.

The more girls I dated, the better I felt. The more people talked about the crazy things Lohman did over the weekend, the bigger I felt. I continually searched for ways to fill the empty hole inside of my soul. Alcohol seemed to fit perfectly.

Living a life without thinking of the consequences governed my daily actions. I had become convinced that I could manipulate my way out of any situation. History had proven so.

Summers at the lake involved tons of booze. This became the norm. Everyone I knew drank like a fish, or so I thought. Drinking a case of beer or downing a bottle of tequila seemed normal to me. Slamming three or four beers down a beer bong to kick off the night helped me enjoy life. Other people were doing it, so why shouldn't I? After all...life is a game about fitting in. Right?

During this period I managed to uphold my "good" image as a sincere and compassionate person. I loved being around family and being available to help anyone who asked. I could turn on and off alcohol depending on the situation. Because I was able to function in this way, I was convinced that alcohol was not yet a problem.

Then the day came when I went to college.

COLLEGE

Wow! No curfew. No parents. No rules, or so I thought. Parties galore. Women plentiful. A chance to create a new identity. Freedom! Freedom!

My drinking became routine from day one. It seemed like everyone in my dorm drank to excess. I lived on a co-ed floor which made it easy to meet tons of girls. Life could not have been better.

Numerous incidents arose from massive consumption of alcohol. The college newspaper repeatedly reported campus incidents that I had participated in, but my name never made into any of the articles. I took pride in this by becoming the Sunday topic around campus.

During my sophomore year the red and blue stopped my buddy and I on our way home from Burger King. Before we knew what had happened we were sleeping on some cots behind some impenetrable steel bars. I called my brother to bail me out but he hung up on me because he thought I was "crying wolf' again, as I had done so many times in the past.

The next day we faced a local judge who sentenced us to take alcohol classes for the rest of the year. I remember the first meeting I attended was full of people my grandparents age talking about all of the "things" they had lost because of alcohol. It was like listening to a country song.

Due to my resentment towards having to attend classes and my lack of desire to stop drinking, I could not relate to the invaluable wisdom being spoken at the alcohol classes. We managed to beat the system and continue our drinking for the duration of that academic year.

Another reason I did not believe in the system was because my probation officer was arrested for trafficking cocaine and the fella running the alcohol classes was arrested for killing someone in a drunk driving accident. These were the people responsible for helping me overcome my drinking? Get real.

I now know that alcohol classes and recovery are the most incredible gifts for an alcoholic of my type.

One last story.

The summer before my senior year of college I almost died, for real this time. It was a typical evening after work. Have a few drinks with friends. Play some pool or darts. Cut a rug on the dance floor. Drive home. That was the usual night. Nothing out of the ordinary.

While driving down the back roads of Michigan a strange event occurred. My tiny little, unclear brain concocted a crazy idea to take out a row of mailboxes on the side of the road. Without thinking of the consequences I proceeded to veer off the road to accomplish the mission. A split second later...mission accomplished. Mailboxes destroyed. Time to head home. Do you think anyone would notice my thrashed hood? Answer is..........of course.

The one thing I forgot to do was consider what was on the other side of the mailboxes. Was it a brick mailbox? No. Was it a house? Thankfully no. Was it a twenty foot drop-off? Unfortunately no. It was a thirty foot drop-off involving a sideways slide for a split second followed by a series of end-over-end flips to eventually land upside down in the middle of some field.

Broken ribs?

Cracked skull?

Fractured leg? Nope.

Just a totaled car and a few minor cuts. Why I did not die that night only God knows, but I am so thankful I am still alive today.   I covered up the accident by saying I swerved to miss a deer. I don't really think anyone believed me. The next few days were quite interesting filled with lies, stories, and deception.   I managed to squander my way out of another potential DUI.

That was the pattern for years to come. So why didn't I just quit drinking?   The answer is simple yet complicated. The simple part is that I lived a life of "yets". I had not yet had a DUI. I had not yet been fired from a job. I had not yet been bankrupt.   I had not yet been divorced. I had not yet started drinking in the morning to get through the day. I had not yet been homeless.   I had not yet physically harmed anyone else. I had not yet...yet....yet. If any of those yets started coming true, then maybe I could have seen the direct results of my drinking.

During this time period I was very aware of my ability to function while under the influence of alcohol. This type of drinker is considered to be a "functional" alcoholic. I didn't always drink to excess. I could put down a full beer and walk away. I could just drink one beer. I could turn on and off my desire to drink around certain people. These episodes of control did occur, but were very infrequent.

POST COLLEGE - The Real World

I will shorten the story by saying that those "yets" I mentioned started coming true. The bad habits I developed in high school and mastered in college continued for the next seven years. My life started spinning out of control faster than I could lower my standards.

Some of the "yets" came true. I was fired from a job due to "poor performance". I did get married and quickly divorced. I did run my finances into the ground as a result of gambling, drinking, and living the good life. I did file for personal bankruptcy.

Suicidal thoughts became plans and almost reality one evening. I had slowly slipped into a depression, a morass of self-pity, or whatever you want to call it. This depression lead me to almost taking my own life on June 7th, 2001.

While drinking with a buddy at a local bar in Fort Wayne, Indiana, an overwhelming feeling came over me that I was finally done drinking. I remember putting down a full beer and saying goodbye to my friends.

Upon arriving home I walked past my dog Jake, placed over three hundred pounds of weights on the barbell of my workout bench, closed my eyes, and was ready to end it all. The ex-wife, the finances, the depression, the everything. I saw the insanity of my life flash before me. I saw the gates of hell.

Just before lift off a warm tingly feeling took over my body. I looked up at Jake and he was doing the dog head tilt thing wondering what his dad was about to do. At that moment a series of questions flew through my brain: Who will feed Jake in the morning? What about my parents? My brother? My friends? What the hell are you doing?

God intervened in the form of my dog. Did you know that dog is God spelled backwards? God pulled me off of that bench, lead me to the kitchen, helped me pour out the rest of my booze, eased my mind, and placed me in his arms for the rest of the evening.

Upon awakening I dialed my parents house to admit out loud that I needed help. We all shed tears of relief and happiness. God removed my obsession and compulsion to drink right then and there. I have not had a drop of booze or any other mind-altering substance since that day. That is a miracle!

~~~~~~

Ever since that day my outlook on life took a one hundred seventy nine degree turn around. My Aunt Carol introduced me to some people just like me. I belonged. I finally belonged!

I discovered a spiritual life beyond comprehension. I learned to wear the world like a loose garment. This sober life allows me to live beyond my comfort zone to actually experience life to the fullest. The "I can't" life transitioned to a "How can I?" life.

Life is now about giving, instead of taking. It is about practicing humility on a daily basis by sharing my experiences with other people. It is about helping someone and not telling anyone about it. It is about looking in the mirror and loving who I see. It is about suiting up and showing up. It is about life.

During the first six months of sobriety I made it through a series of extremely difficult events including the death of my grandmother Nana, the death of my grandfather Bopps, filing for divorce, filing for bankruptcy, being fired from a job, relocating to a new city…. Those were all great excuses to drink over, but the thought of alcohol never occurred. God had removed my mental obsession and physical compulsion of alcohol.

With the help of others who were living a sober life, I now knew that life without alcohol was possible. What a gift to live a sober life. What a gift to live life with a conscious contact with God founded by faith.

Do you remember that scene in Indiana Jones and The Last Crusade when Indi needed to take a "leap of faith" across a ravine in order to save his dying father? There was no evidence of a bridge, it seemed impossible. Uncertain he would survive, Indi knew he must believe or his father would die. Indi took that first spiritual step of faith and found that the bridge or pathway to his goal always existed. He just lacked the faith.

Upon returning to his father, Indi encountered the ravine once again. This time he had the faith and crossed the bridge in confidence. That pretty much sums up my walk of faith. I, just like Indi, believe the pathway always exists, even if I cannot directly see the physical evidence.

The best way to describe how I try to live life today is through series of prayers I use throughout my days. I start my day with the Serenity Prayer followed by quiet times of meditation. This helps focus the day through God's eyes. My favorite is the Prayer of Saint Francis.

"Lord, make me a channel of thy peace - that where there is hatred, I may bring love - that where there is wrong, I may bring the spirit of forgiveness - that where there is discord, I may bring harmony - that where there is error, I may bring truth - that where there is doubt, I may bring faith - that where there is despair, I may bring hope - that where there are shadows, I may bring light - that where there is sadness, I may bring joy. Lord, grant that I may seek rather to comfort than to be comforted - to understand, than to be understood - to love, than to be loved. For it is by self-forgetting that one finds. It is by forgiving that one is forgiven. It is by dying that one awakens to the Eternal Life. Amen."

The author of the above prayer was a man who for several hundred years now has been rated as a saint. Although he was not an alcoholic, he did, like me, go through the emotional wringer. And as he came out the other side of that painful experience, the above prayer was his expression of what he could then see, feel, and wish to become.

I don't know about you, but to live a life as described by Saint Francis is the ultimate achievement.   Until then, I'll do my best.   I would ask you to do the same.

Thank you for reading about the real me. I would be happy to receive emails or comments from anyone concerned about a loved one or yourself regarding alcohol. There is help for those who want help.
Feel free to send any confidential emails of concern to me at 179degrees@themomentumjourney.org.